More to MY Life

by More to her Life charity

First published by More to her Life charity
www.moretoherlife.co.uk

© 2021 Victoria Padmore

Paperback ISBN: 978-1-7399850-0-4

Cover design and typesetting: Fuzzy Flamingo
www.fuzzyflamingo.co.uk

This book is dedicated to women across the world.

Women who haven't been able to escape their abuse relationships yet,
Women who continue in the cycle of abusive relationships,
Women who didn't survive and never had the chance to build their
own incredible lives away from abuse.

These are all our sisters and I dedicate this book to them
with all my love.

Contents

Introduction

Welcome to *More to MY Life* published by More to her Life charity. *More to MY Life* is a collection of life stories from women who have experienced domestic abuse. The chapters you will find here focus on their experiences as they leave abusive relationships and how they have rebuilt their lives.

I am so excited, honoured and humbled to introduce you to the incredible women in this book. Each one of these women have experienced domestic abuse, have found the strength to leave and then have created an incredible life away from abuse. Creating an incredible life means something different to each of them; it could be an incredible love, an incredible business or being incredibly supportive to other women. However, what is most important and true for each of them is that they are incredibly happy, incredibly secure and incredibly confident in themselves. That is what makes theirs an incredible life.

I also want to thank you! That is the most important thing I want to say to you in this introduction: Thank you!

You will find the women in this book inspiring regardless of what your personal circumstances are, but also, when buying this book, you have gifted another copy to a woman living in a domestic abuse refuge right now. For her, she is at the beginning of her journey and these stories hold a different significance for her. You have gifted inspiration, and you have gifted hope that she too can create an incredible life away from abuse. This gift that you have purchased could ripple out and change every aspect of her life forever. On average, a woman will leave an abusive partner eight times before she leaves for good. Some women living in refuges have tried several times before to leave and heartbreakingly some women living in refuges will go back to their partners.

I firmly believe a huge contributing factor is the fear of the unknown future. When leaving an abusive relationship, often women lose every aspect of their lives and have to rebuild everything. This, along with the fact that previously their partner has controlled every aspect of their lives, means that women find it incredibly difficult to imagine how their lives will be moving forward. The fear of the unknown often feels worse to them than the life they have just left.

This book is to show women leaving abusive relationships that life moving forward can be incredible, this is not their defining moment, there is so much more to come. To move forward, women need to believe that their future will be better than life with an abusive partner.

This book could be the start of that belief for the woman your book is gifted to.

If you are reading this book and you are thinking of leaving an abusive relationship or have just left and abusive relationship or are still healing years later, I want to thank you for also buying this inspiration and hope for yourself. Domestic abuse has been a part of your life, as it has for all the women in this book, and it is a life changing part, but don't let it be the defining chapter when you look back on your life. You will see, as you read through this book, domestic abuse has had an impact on each of these women's lives; however, they have gone on to create many incredible moments, achievements and entire lives that bring them great joy and completely overshadow the abuse they experienced in their life story.

I hope this book inspires you with the life you can build yourself. What you do in your life each day is no longer someone else's choice. What you want long term is no longer someone else's want. You are moving on to a new chapter and you have the power to write it. Each woman in this book has at one point experienced what it is like to escape an abusive relationship, and some explain these moments within their chapters; you may relate to them with how you are feeling right now. Whilst you relate to these moments, just remember they have gone on to build incredible lives.

As you read through each chapter, you will be introduced to a range of different life experiences; however, you will notice that at the core of what has helped each woman is reconnecting with who they are and what they want from their own lives.

This is why at the end of each chapter you will find a section to reflect on what you felt whilst reading that chapter and how you can take their experiences to help you move forward in your own life. This writing is what a lot of people refer to as journaling. Journaling is simply writing out your own thoughts to help make sense of them. I'm sure you have often felt overwhelmed with so many thoughts and emotions held in your head. Journaling helps you get these thoughts and emotions out and on to paper where we can process them better and help us start to work through them. The chapters in this book will bring up emotions and thoughts and the journaling sections in this book are for you to start to make sense of these emotions. You can use the questions the authors have written to help you get started or you can just start writing about what you felt.

Being able to connect with your own thoughts, wants and desires is so very important and I truly hope the journaling space in this book helps you to do this.

Thank you again for your purchase and for your gift to another woman. You may need to hear these stories yourself to make changes you need to in your own life, you may just enjoy the stories of strength and growth, you may have an incredible story yourself. Wherever you are in your own life, I hope you enjoy and celebrate these women and the inspiration they are whilst knowing you are supporting a woman living in a refuge.

If after reading these incredible life stories you would like to meet more inspirational women who have created incredible lives away from abuse please visit www. moretoherlife.co.uk/incrediblelives to read more stories

Thanks

I would also like to take this opportunity to truly thank each and every woman who contributed to this book. It is never easy to relive elements of your life that brought so much pain but I am truly thankful that these women took time to share their experiences from a place of love and truly wanting to support other women.

Once you have built a life away from abuse the difference you feel in every aspect of your life is so dramatic and incredible that you have a real desire to see other women make the same changes which is why they agreed to be part of this book. Some of the women involved regularly share their experience and others have done so for the first time, each time it takes a lot of time and emotional energy to share and be inspirational.

I will always be eternally grateful for the words they have shared and the love they have spread.

Thanks also goes to Nicole Cherie Barker who fully funded this project and made it possible to publish this book and gift it to you. Nicole is an incredible ongoing supporter of More to her Life charity both through her business, as a trustee and as a dear friend. Nicole has created an incredible life for her and her children by anyone's standards, and when she shares the experiences of her past it makes her accomplishments even more incredible. Nicole changes lives daily through her business coaching where mindset and self assurance is the cornerstone of everything.

I will let Nicole share with you why she wanted to fund this book personally.

"The clouds are white and fluffy against the crystal blue water below. The world looks so small from all the way up here. I'm on my way to Florida to attend a Mastermind meeting with an elite group of seven and eight figure entrepreneurs – flying first class. The little cheese snacks and almonds are delicious. I'm still a little suspicious of how nice the flight attendant is, but when I stare at the man sleeping next to me, a big breath of peace flows all the way in and all the way out. I close my eyes and pinch myself, because it wasn't always this way…

Less than four years ago, I was on a very different flight, with a very different man. In the back of the plane, trying not to wake him up for fear of the fight that would surely ensue. My passport was tucked safely in his bag, far out of my reach. I kept my head down, afraid that someone would notice my swollen lip – which was nothing compared to the anxiety that ripped through my chest, tying my intestines in rage-filled knots. The bruises were like sweet little strawberry shortcakes compared to the apocalyptic war zone in my mind. The terror ransacked my dreams and relentlessly stole away any hope for rest.

A lot can change in a very short amount of time.

A swell of gratitude washes over me now. I can feel my heart pitter-pattering along, singing a sweet little song, like a spring time swallow sitting on the window sill, happiness bursts through me and I can't help but smile at strangers. Alive. I feel alive. And so happy for it.

Victoria Padmore was my second client when I started my brand new business. I really had to twist her arm to get her into my program. We talked a lot and for a long while before I could finally convince her to *come join the land of unicorns. I just had to have her. Sweet bubbly little smile. And an English accent is enough to make any American swoon. Fast friends, but both guarded from the overlapping stories of our past. She had the most lovely concept when she joined my online program that teaches entrepreneurs how to use social media strategies to sell their programs, products or services.*

Victoria was selling a book. Well, actually, a diary. It was called My Compliment Diary and it was all about empowering other women in your life. You could get one for your mother or sister or friend. Or you could get one for yourself. Which was a really intriguing concept to me. I was terrible at accepting compliments from others and I sure as hell didn't give them to myself!

From the beginning, Victoria had big dreams. Dreams that were often stifled by what was "realistic". I've always hated that word. It makes me laugh now. It isn't "realistic" for a woman who has lived my life to be making six figures a month while engaged to the love of her life, raising two happy and healthy teenage children. Yet, here I am. So when Victoria told me she wanted to start a charity, I was all for it. Screw realistic, let's swing for the fence! You see, Victoria has an incredible heart. She is a true unicorn. She did the work. She put in the hours, untangled all of the red tape and pushed through the tears until her charity, her dream, was more than realistic… It was a reality!

When she asked me to be a trustee, I cried. The fact that she trusted me, that she wanted me, that she saw my value, that moment changed everything for me. More than she will ever know. I'm holding back the tears right now thinking about the true impact of that question. My past has the propensity to haunt me. And at times, I can't believe what I went through. But knowing that I get to have a seat next to this incredibly heart-centered woman while she tirelessly serves, supports and empowers women who are stepping out of their old lives and into their new ones… well, if I wasn't writing a chapter for this book, I would tell you there are no words.

It is a glittery sparkle in my chest. It's teal and prismatic. It looks like the toothpaste that's on the box, not the real life toothpaste, smudgy and dull, the perfectly pretty one on the commercials! It's the sensation of being minty fresh and new. That same feeling of being truly ALIVE.

It's the feeling that I GET to be here – Which wasn't always a likely outcome.

I get to donate my time, my energy, my expertise and of course, my money to More to her Life. I get to be a part of something bigger than myself. I get to know how far I have come, to really see it, to really feel it, by being a part of this program. When Victoria told me that she wanted to write a collaboration book, I didn't wait for her to ask someone else. Honestly, I didn't even wait for her to ask me, I immediately jumped on board and funded the project because this is so incredibly important.

When I look back at where I was and what would have helped me in those moments, on that flight, I think about the notion that maybe, just maybe, I would have stumbled on that book after he finally got arrested. Maybe I would have read a story from one of these incredible women and thought to myself, I can do this. Maybe I would have felt my heart stir, just like it is right now writing this. Maybe something in me would have woken up faster. Maybe I wouldn't have spent so long suffering. Maybe I would have found my hope much sooner than I did. Maybe I could have gotten that time back with my children. Maybe I would have stopped crying *sooner. Everything worked out incredibly well. It really did. So I don't want to complain. I did what I needed to do. And I'm so happy now, so fulfilled, so in love with my new life and the person that I see in the mirror. But it did take quite a long time. They are all days that I can't get back.*

In my business, I am always telling my clients, success loves speed, momentum is key, keep going, don't let anything stop you! And I guess that is because that is what I kept telling myself when I finally got out. Don't look back. Don't let anything stop you. You got this!

If I only knew how many people would eventually rally behind me. If I only knew how much love and support I would receive from perfect strangers on the internet. If I only knew who I would become just a few short years later, I would have suffered a whole lot less knowing that my future would be so wonderfully bright. And that is why I am here. That is why this book matters to me. That is why each of these women who are donating their time, their energy and sharing their inspirational stories matter so much to me. That is why Victoria matters so much to me. Because now I know, there was always so much more to my life. And I want you to know that is true for you too. This is just the beginning."

I will now pass over to my incredible co-authors who are excited to share their experiences with you. They are excited for you to start connecting with the freedom, happiness and stability that a life away from abuse will bring you.

Victoria x

Love, Money, Mind:

my secret to healing from past abuse

Anna Davidson

It took five years and thirty-two court cases to gain my legal freedom from my now ex-husband. But my journey to personal freedom and full control of my life started the moment I finally realised the enormity of the wrongness that was happening to me. With my eyes finally wide open, I immediately began to prepare for my exit plan – and then I left him. Or rather, I escaped from him. With our two beautiful, innocent boys and a few worldly belongings, the years of incessant energy-sapping adrenaline and new-found focused determination and courage carried me wordlessly and emotionlessly away from the silently closed front door of our marital home, and into my getaway car. I knew that this journey – to somewhere, to anywhere – was to be the ultimate escape from indescribable pain: never again would my chosen path lead back to him and the source of my pain. Never again would I look backwards. This was now my time, and my turn to live; I had to make it happen. To help me survive and thrive, I focused on three words: love, money and mind. This is my story of how this focus helps me – and now others – heal from the victimisation of past abuse.

Love

When my journey towards freedom began, my priority focus was – and still is – love. I do not mean romantic love – or seeking love from others, in the hope of feeling better in myself – but looking inwards, searching out and acknowledging the huge empty voids that lurked there, filling their sad hollowness with love and self-care. At the start of my journey, loving myself was certainly a tall order for someone like me, and how I then perceived myself: a bright, loving, vivacious and driven perfectionist who had failed. I blamed myself for the love he could and would not give me. Self-care and self-love, I came to learn, were not about being or trying to be a perfect person, but about loving myself unconditionally.

I knew that I had to pick up my self-esteem and self-worth from where I had last felt them within me, many years beforehand. Feeling numb and exhausted, it was up to me to brush off the vestiges of how I once valued myself; up to me to work hard at pulling the weak dregs of my once worthiness together; up to me to fix them together, and to build them up into the new, unfettered me I was yet to discover. I also knew that this resolve to love and heal myself would not prove an easy journey. But, more importantly, I instinctively knew that nothing along my new journey towards freedom would be more difficult than what I had already been through.

The relationship was over in my head the minute I left it. Yet, learning to love myself immediately came up against a number of frustrating challenges. Now I know that these obstacles of trauma that taunted me along my road to recovering self-love are normal for victims of domestic abuse. But I did not want to normalise them in my new life. All too often the obstacles stopped me suddenly and unpredictably in my determined tracks, holding me down with motionless sobbing, and with frantic, chest-stabbing and shirt-soaked anxiety. Along with the sighing and pensive euphoria of a new escapee, I also felt down, alone and in an emotional state.

And the obstacles to learning to love myself were immense: I lost a significant amount of weight – and also some friends – as I faced and replayed the cruelty and trauma of the past, over and over again, for each of the thirty-two court cases I had to prepare for and attend in his presence. People I needed to understand my situation did not: support services and friends vocally expressed their unrequested, skewed and ignorant perceptions of a comfortable and happy lifestyle that I portrayed; one that they incorrectly assumed that I could have easily walked away from at any time – and why hadn't I? I quickly had to learn to accept that behind-doors manipulation, coercion and control – and strangled screams of agony, and vain cries for help – cannot be readily seen on the falsely loyal, yet shamed and embarrassed faces of the perpetrators' victims, who eventually (and hopefully) emerge gasping from the all-too-often gaslit confines of the four walls loosely and numbly termed 'home'. I had to learn that some of those people who were then closest to me would never believe me – and that I had to let them go.

Acknowledging and accepting what had happened to me was a big step towards loving myself. I used social media platforms to talk about the abuse, which I know embarrassed those people close to me, their stiff-upper-lipped generational distance making the public disclosure uncomfortable for them. However, my mission to help others has always been bigger than the image of victim – the branding – that I have inadvertently given myself online. And so, I continued with communicating in this way because I remain convinced that, by doing so, the empathy and solidarity empower others to take positive action for themselves, and thus to take action against their abusers. In social media, I had also found a medium of expressing and respecting my own experiences and feelings. This was the beginnings of self-love for me.

But I also had to work out an exit plan of action – of survival – and the urgency of this kept me moving forward. I knew that all I really needed was a handful of supportive, loving people beside me, which I was blessed to have had. I wanted him to be part of that exit plan, for the sake of our two boys, but my honourable intention just did not work out. So, I realised that I had to focus on me, and searching out, and loving, all my strengths and capabilities. While I had made little steps towards love on my own, I realised that I would also need someone beside me, holding my hand, encouraging me to keep walking forwards, occasionally carrying me, while I worked out how to face and circumvent the often horrific obstacles along the way.

I chose talking therapy – and a wonderful therapist. Talk therapy, which is also known as psychotherapy, is what mental health professionals use to communicate with their patients. The purpose of talk therapy is to help people identify issues that cause emotional distress. With her, I learned not to fight my emotions, but to allow them, and to let the trapped negative energy out into the open. I learned that therapist rooms with the obligatory box of tissues on their pristine coffee tables do not symbolise personal weakness on the part of the domestic and sexual abuse victim – nor that I had failed and arrived at the last resort. Counselling proved to be an important part of my journey to discover love. And I learned to accept and love myself completely. The blame and shame began to wane, as I began to understand my past, and all its many red flags that had been foisted on me and my misplaced empathy. I began to use the far too lengthy court process – in itself used as a medium for his control over me – as a means to offload my thoughts, memories and emotions, and to lean on available support. I gave myself permission to accept and encourage my self-development, and to ensure that my mindset continued to develop positively. I began to stand back and recover from years of relentless, obsessive harassment.

I am now extremely, and perhaps oddly, grateful for having experienced the abuse, and for learning from it: I am a different person. Once a party animal, masking the pain with blank smiles and boozy dancing, paradoxically my journey of recovery has given me a lot of time on my own, and I have got to know and love myself very well; loneliness has fortified my inner strength. Now, I am rarely conscious of the anxiety and anger that occasionally take a joyride with my otherwise enlivened and enthusiastic soul.

My time – my space – is all about a self-care routine now: a week of work and quality time with my boys, and strict Saturday morning chill-outs, where the diary is blanked out specifically, a long breakfast ending the ritual, leading into fun-filled family time for the rest of the day. I meditate daily, both guided (by someone else), and on my own, which is important for those of us working in the digital world, but also for me maintaining a peaceful work-life balance, and an unbroken process of continued recovery, health and happiness. I love to bathe each night – early, and with a glass of wine. I always shut my brain off before I go to sleep. Sleep – and plenty of it – remains a priority.

It was only by learning and consistently practising self-love and self-care – and really believing in myself, and my self-worth – that I began to build up my self-esteem, self-confidence and positive energy levels. I also found a purpose in life that was bigger than helping myself; I eventually felt that I had the capacity to pass on the love to others, and to help and empower other women. My goal now is to impact a million women globally with my story. No small feat, but because I know the potential value of my story in helping others, I really believe this can be achieved.

For me, an extremely important part of passing on the love, is being an ambassador for the domestic abuse charity The Buddy Bag Foundation (https://buddybagfoundation. co.uk/). The charity helps people who have to flee to refuge centres because of the domestic abuse they experience. I heard about it on Facebook, and one day made a decision to approach the charity myself. For a few months, and in readiness for a quick escape from the marital home with my children, I had my Buddy Bag containing items I might need in an emergency locked away in the boot of my car. Part of my journey of recovery from domestic abuse has been in giving some goodness to others, so making the best use of all the bad that happened to me. Being part of such a worthy charity is my way of giving back.

So many women have sent me stories of what they've been through, and they thank me for speaking out. I genuinely believe that my story of past abuse has given me an important mission in life: to support and proudly inspire other women entrepreneurs in pursuit of their own business dreams, just as I have done so for myself. I also understood that about 60% of women want to run their own online business, but fear stops them. To spread the word, and to pass on the love, I now teach others how to emulate my online business success as an Amazon entrepreneur (and for more about that, see below). I also recently released my book, entitled *She Made It Happen*, which tells the stories of fifteen inspirational women, all of whom have turned their painful past stories into personal successes. My eBook, called *The 5 Steps To Sell Professionally on Amazon*, as well as a course and coaching programme 'Amazon 101 Academy' together with a membership site I have created for potential entrepreneurs, called 'Make Sh★t Happen', also have the primary aim of reaching out to and inspiring as many women on their personal journeys as possible. Motivated by my own success as a domestic and sexual abuse survivor and thriver, I launched 'Your Freedom Podcast', in which I interview my guests to share their stories about love, money and mind – the three topics I focus on, and which helped me get back some equilibrium in my life.

Money

I am running away with myself. What I have not told you is how, in learning to love myself – and, ultimately, in sharing that love with others – I threw myself into my business as a healing process. I had to focus on money, as well as love. And just as I learned to live my life with the guidance of my talking therapist counsellor, two other people were particularly inspirational in the money part of my journey to freedom. At the beginning of my journey, I had been part of the high-action, all-consuming corporate world for sixteen years, earning the reputation as The Viagra Rep. I was doing exceptionally well: I had a company car and substantial bonuses. I had, and personally paid for, the lifestyle everyone envied: the big house, the exotic holidays, the flamboyant parties. But it was all superficial, lying on the surface, with cracks starting to appear. Life had become monotonous, and time beyond work was limited. The feeling of needing to escape a highly toxic relationship was growing within me, as was my need to leave the extreme demands of my job: my income was capped, but the far-too-many hours I gave my employer were not; I was frequently away from home, and I yearned to be with my two young boys.

My entrepreneurial streak was alive and kicking, and I wanted to live a life with more meaning, more purpose. But I did not know where to start: my failed marriage had completely eroded my self-confidence. At this stage, my two focuses of love and money were too big to handle, and I felt that I could not go on. My inner voice, however, urged me to get up, sort myself out, and help others like me. Amongst the defeatism and depression I was experiencing, the little voice of knowledge telling me that I could completely change my life screamed loud and clear to me. But I could not see how I could change my life: I had no relevant skills nor qualifications to help people, and who would listen to me, anyway? And then I was made redundant from my job, and all roads to learn and gain confidence seemed blocked to me. And so, I did nothing.

An online entrepreneur added me as a friend on Facebook. His life looked enviable: he lived life on his own terms; he drove a Lamborghini; he travelled the world –

and he was ten years younger than me. We had similar backgrounds, though: he, too, had worked in the corporate world, and I could fully relate to his need to escape from the rat race. As I read more about him, I felt my subdued self-confidence grow: I could do this, too. He sent me a message, inviting me to a webinar. My inner voice made me sign up to it. My desires for a new life urged me on: I not only wanted to earn the same six-figure-a-month income – but also to help people change their lives, by encouraging them to change their mindsets of limiting beliefs. I felt both excited and scared. But I knew I had to work with him.

From there, I wanted to learn more about digital marketing. At that stage of my journey to freedom, Blockbusters – an American-based provider of home movie and video game rental services – had just gone into receivership in the UK. In its wake, Netflix – a streaming service offering a wide variety of award-winning TV shows, movies, anime, documentaries, and so on – was just taking off. I could see that we were on a new wave of a digital economy, and I needed to learn the relevant skills so I could be part of this new digital world. I was nervous, but keen to learn and make a difference in the world.

I focused my attention on Facebook and Amazon. I realised that both these platforms could provide a means to market and to sell goods: everyone was by then shopping online. The way we communicated was changing, and the internet was there for the grabbing. At the same time, I could see that businesses were not prepared to take full advantage of this new digital age, and their sales were flagging as a result. I knew I had to be part of the scene, driving the change.

I started out by learning more about Facebook. It was becoming huge and having a considerable impact on people's lives. But I could see that it was also important for selling products, as well as personal brand building. With the power of paid Facebook advertising, online brands could profit significantly.

I also started selling products on Amazon, using their marketplace through 'Fulfilment By Amazon' (also known as Amazon FBA). Partnering with Amazon was truly amazing: I decided on a niche (for example, sports and fitness), then created brands of physical products within this niche. I sourced these products from suppliers in China and sent my new creations to Amazon's warehouse. Amazon would then take care of the rest: picking and packing my products direct to the customer, and managing customer services and returns, while I focused on the marketing and selling of my physical product brands. I then sent my unique product lines to the USA, UK and across Europe, sometimes not having seen the actual physical product myself.

With my confidence growing, I then created a partnership with someone I met online, who had been importing from China for many years by then. Together, we created an offline workshop, teaching students how to import from China and sell on Amazon Marketplace. Using the new digital skills I had acquired, I set up an online coaching business, gained new clients, and began to make very good money. But I had not fully achieved what I had set out to do on my new journey to freedom. I was still trading time for money, just as in my previous job as The Viagra Rep. I was still trying to juggle business with children and, at the same time as I was finding love and healing from an abusive relationship, I was also finding that I was losing touch with reality: I was not present, and always felt under pressure – and was extremely exhausted. I burned out. My flexibility, freedom and happiness were being compromised by the business model of coaching on a one-to-one basis online, as well as running offline workshops. My time was not my own, and yet I convinced myself that because I worked from home, I was also available for my two boys. In reality, I was helping my clients more than I was my boys. My purpose in life, too, was evasive: I was not making the impact I had set out to achieve. I played with the idea of returning to the corporate world, but my inner voice yelled at me again: I knew I was close to achieving my desires, despite not being able to see or feel them. I had learned so much about the new digital world, and I, and my new-found skills, were not prepared to give up yet. I had gained so much control over my life by then that I really could not see myself handing that freedom over to someone managing me in the corporate world.

And so, I persisted. I decided that I needed to be very clear about what it was that I really wanted: to travel more overseas, and to make more memories for myself and my two boys. As a single parent, I wanted my children to see the world, and to get inspired for their own futures, too. I also wanted to run online courses, and to be with my kids – and be fully present with them – every day. I wanted to be a mum who never missed a sports day; was always there to pick them up from school; had the time to make cakes with them, or get the paints out and be creative with them. I wanted and needed to be part of their stories, as much as they are part of mine. I also wanted to inspire other women like me: mums who want a limitless income, and who want to travel the world, while at the same time optimising their time with their children. A female entrepreneur I had followed on social media for a while invited me to a seminar she was speaking at for women in business. I had done a lot of networking with women and mumpreneurs, but had become tired of the 'boss-woman' types. I had noted that they were unduly competitive with each other, and constantly ran each other down with judgmental negativities. But this woman entrepreneur was different. She was really inspirational in her proactivity, refusing to respond to adversity and hostility, and I highly respected that she respected other women. Speaking to a room of 200 people, this woman entrepreneur shared how her son had died from cancer, and how she then built a seven-figure online business through courses. She had a powerful story, and the people listening to her bought into her and her courses because of it. This event helped me get focused, and inspired me to reach out to her; she became my coach. I could see then that if I shared my own story and got it out into the world, it would also become a vehicle to inspire others. Yes, I wanted financial freedom, but I also yearned to get my awful and horrendous domestic abuse story out beyond the social media platforms and my talking therapist, too. I wanted to help others beyond my immediate circle, who were in the same situation as I had been; I wanted to help them escape. I also wanted to inspire those wanting to start an online business: if I could do it against all odds, then so could they. If I could get on the stage and tell my story, help people start a business on Amazon and make six-figure incomes and more, then I could also step up a level and have more impact in the world.

The next day, I came up with a new course idea. I added all the people I had connected with at the women's business event, and also connected with a celebrity. I announced my new course the following week and had a pre-launch offer. That week, I made £10,000 and, for the first time, I felt so clear in my intentions. I had a simple game plan; I was focused; I was no longer trading time for money. I now had the potential to reach thousands of other people who wanted to learn from me, and so could make a huge impact in the world, with a real sense of purpose: to help other mums, dads, or anybody who wanted freedom and true flexibility to run an online business. I also now had the freedom and money to travel overseas whenever I wanted to with my boys. I have had an impact on thousands of people's lives through my online courses and joint ventures and can earn as much as I want with no limit on my income. Just before the Covid-19 lockdown in March 2020, I travelled to China, Hong Kong, Singapore, Miami, the Caribbean and

Portugal, and had plans for more. So, with love and money focused upon throughout my journey towards freedom, what am I now, at the end of it? I am proud and humbled to say that I am an eCommerce and digital marketing expert, author, mumpreneur, founder of Amazon 101 Academy, and have created a community of Amazon Queens. I became an Amazon seller in 2013, and have since taught over 2000 students to build successful businesses through on and offline training programs. I have a passion for branding and turning seemingly ordinary products into unique lines. I have built multiple brands from scratch with years of online marketing experience. I have a knack for being able to rank quickly on Amazon, and for outsmarting the competition. A self-taught digital marketing guru, I featured in *Forbes* magazine in April 2020 about how to sell successfully online. I pinch myself constantly. But as an internationally award-winning businesswoman, I also give back as much as possible, by offering free marketing advice and business coaching to other potential entrepreneurs, many of whom are also overcoming their own adversities. I do this through a podcast, membership site and books. My first book *She Made It Happen* retells the inspirational stories of fifteen women who, like me, have turned adversity into personal success.

So, despite coming up against many entrepreneurial and personal challenges during my journey from abuse to freedom, I managed to start my own business – and changed my life forever.

Mind

Love, money and – last but not least – mind. It is our mind that limits our beliefs. This is where Fred in the Head lives: he is everything that we tell ourselves. And he tells us some porkies, believe me! He stops us doing what we need and want to do, by playing with our heads and putting doubt and insecurities into our minds. He leaves us worried and insecure. Fred in the Head is clingy, and still sticks around for me. I notice him when sometimes I find that my head is back in the past, and I am feeling angry at my ex-husband for not being a father to the boys; for making me pay financially and emotionally for the abuse I was subjected to.

For the first couple of years of my journey to freedom, I felt worthless; not good enough; it was all my fault. That was Fred in the Head tricking me. Occasionally, I still feel fear. A loud, unexplained bang outside the house opens the floodgates to unwelcome and horrific memories of being stalked and harassed outside my home, leaving me quaking, and shouting hard in my head at Fred in the Head to go away. But, ultimately, harassment charges, court battles and injunctions over the last few years did not impede my efforts to pursue independence and build on my business education. This was down to ignoring Fred in the Head and, instead, adopting a new and positive mindset. I believe that we all have a purpose in this world. We all have a voice – and the skills, capability, experience and knowledge – to help others in such a positive way.

We all want understanding, we all want belief and, more importantly, we all want happiness to live a successful, purposeful, time-freedom life. I left my employment and became financially free. But only because I stepped out of my past and out of my comfort zone – knowing that life could only get better. I think what happened to me, happened because I am an empathetic person; I absorbed cruelty unquestioningly, by attempting to understand and excuse its source. Now, I use my empathetic nature to help all those women who have been smothered by the red flags of abuse that they did not see coming. The abuse did not make us strong; I do not believe that. We have overcome the abuse because we are already strong. I believe that my mission is to help us survivors truly believe this.

And because of my mission – my changed mindset – my mantra is now 'freedom': I am free to be able to do what I want to do, and to create a life that I want. Happiness, born out of freedom, is when what we think, what we say and what we do are all aligned in harmony. My pain has become my power: I feel as though I have found a meaning in the suffering. I focus on making more of my future – with love, money, mind – and not making much of my lost time.

For too many tortuous years, I was the silent victim of indescribable domestic and sexual abuse. I lost my voice, my identity, my sense of life purpose; I had been reduced to nothing. A loving mum of two young sons, I have since empowered myself, not only to overcome the effects of the abuse as best as I can, but also to continue to work on being the best possible version of myself. My once suppressed and traumatised silence now proudly shouts out loud that I am a thriver: I have overcome torture and adversity to become an internationally award-winning businesswoman. As a now world-renowned and inspirational entrepreneur, my mission, as a survivor of extreme coercive and controlling behaviour, is to encourage like-minded women to achieve their own dreams and routes to financial independence. I help women like me to overcome their own deep-seated pain and personal fears, and to discover their own voices and inner strengths for themselves. I made it happen!

To know more about Anna and her advocacies, visit: theannadavidson.com
Subscribe to her YouTube channel – Anna Davidson
Join her tribe on Your Freedom Project Facebook group and get connected with amazing people.

Use this space to journal:

Journal questions:

1. What self-care routine could you work into every day? Even if it is a few moments to start with.
2. List all the jobs you have had and think of all the skills they taught you.
3. What lies does your "Fred in the Head" tell you? Now scribble it all out and know that he is lying!

_____

_____

_____

_____

_____

_____

_____

_____

_____

_____

_____

_____

_____

I Was Finally Living My Dream Life and It Felt So Good

Donna Liddle

While I hadn't planned to leave that particular day, I had been trying to prepare myself for when that day would come.

I was finally admitting to myself that I was unhappy in the relationship. It felt like it was killing me to be there. I was beginning to see how different we were and how different our ideas of the future looked. He had always said he couldn't give me what I wanted, and, for the first time, I knew it for myself. It was going to be tough to end things, but it had to happen.

I was going to be forty years old later that year and I knew I couldn't reach forty and still be living this life. I was psyching myself up to leave, telling myself I could do it.

When we got into an argument that day, something inside me shifted and I knew that it was now or never. I was telling myself, 'This is it, it's time to go.' I packed all of my stuff and I left. This was the time I was leaving, and I was never going back.

I was trying so hard to believe that this was really it. I'd lost count of how many times I had packed my things, left and then gone back. I've read that on average it takes a person eight times to leave an abusive relationship before it is final, and I can absolutely see how it takes so many times.

Sometimes I was only gone for a matter of hours before I would go back. In fact, I think the longest I had previously lasted was about a week before I fell for the charm and believed it would all be different this time, and slowly but surely went back.

There were those times when I would leave and then convince myself that I was just overreacting and go back after a few hours feeling a bit stupid for making such a big deal of the situation. We would have the usual talk where we'd each make promises and try to figure out how to make things better between us.

There were times where I was determined that was it, I wasn't ever going back. Then he seemed to have this way of drawing me back in. I have no idea how he did it. We would go through this whole rigmarole where he'd message me, I would try hard to ignore him. Then he would be really nasty, then nice, then back to nasty when nice didn't work.

Eventually I would start to feel bad and then he would say something that would hook me back in. We'd start talking again. Then came the promises that everything would change. He'd tell me everything that I so badly wanted to hear. He'd tell me how much he loved me and wanted me. It was such a toxic relationship.

Of course, I'd go back, things would change for a short

time, and we would both try a little harder for a while. He would turn on the charm, be more loving, do things he knew would make me happy, showing me how much of an effort he was making to change. Eventually it would go back to the way it always was.

I remember saying to myself as I moved my things back, that last time, 'The next time I leave I won't ever be coming back.' I guess I knew I needed to leave for good, but it just wasn't as simple as that.

Each time that I left and went back, I so badly wanted things to be different, I believed and hoped every single time that they would be. Sadly, the reality is, I always found that they weren't, and I guess one day I realised they never ever would be.

When I left this time, it was different. We went through the usual dance, the nastiness, the promises, that things will be different. This time the thing that was different was me. This was the last time and so I kept telling myself there was no going back. This had to be it.

I had been building my strength for this moment for over a year (since the last time I left and went back). No matter what, I just needed to stay strong. I knew it wasn't going to be easy, but I really wasn't prepared for how things turned out.

For a month, things were all over the place and – no surprise – in that time I even went back. There was a bit of an incident and through fear of things turning very nasty I tried to calm the situation. Agreeing to go back felt like the only way to do that, so I told him we could give it another go.

I lasted a week, and I really just couldn't stay. I was frightened of him, I didn't really want to be near him or for him to touch me. This just wasn't going to work, I needed it to be over. It was time to break this cycle and get out for good.

We were still in touch and, during the weeks that followed, I thought we had managed to get to a good place. I felt things were going to be amicable between us. That was short-lived before everything blew up. After finding out I had spent time with a male friend, the situation escalated, and I feared for my own safety and the safety of my friend. I had no choice, I had to involve the police.

Looking back, I was so naïve; at no point had I ever anticipated that things would get to that stage. I honestly believed I could just walk away, like I had from other relationships, and that we'd stay friends. I never for a second imagined that I would have to get the police involved or that I would have to go to court to get a non-molestation order.

The strength I found to leave was nothing like the strength I had to find to get through the following months.

At times I felt like I was completely losing it and that I wasn't strong enough to cope and get through it. I was terrified of what might happen, while at the same time I was trying to process what had actually been happening in the relationship. I began to question everything I had believed about myself and my relationship. I couldn't get my head around what was going on.

I had absolutely no idea who I was or how in the hell I was ever going to get through it.

I had pretty much lived in a constant state of anxiety

throughout our whole relationship, but everything that I was going through and trying to deal with took that anxiety to a whole new level.

At first, I was terrified to go anywhere for fear of being seen. For what felt like forever all I wanted to do was hide myself away. I actually tried to initially, although quite unsuccessfully as he very quickly found me.

Representing myself and having to come face-to-face with him in court was one of the most difficult things I have done. I was in pieces. I remember standing in the toilets trying to pull myself together, telling myself I could do it. I am still not sure where that strength came from for me to get through that, but I am so proud of myself that I did it. I was finally standing up for myself.

Once the non-molestation order was in place, I began to push myself to start getting my life back to some kind of normality. Life felt far from normal. I had changed all of my routines, adjustments were made at work, especially so I was never in the office or leaving work alone. I drove different routes to work so I had less chance of being seen.

I constantly questioned myself: 'How is this my life now?' I was supposed to be free.

There were times I believed that it was never ever going to end. I couldn't cope with how bad the situation was and how the ever-increasing fear and anxiety were making me feel. It was all too much. I needed it all to stop. It wasn't just having an impact on my life but it was having an impact on the lives of those around me and the relationships with those close to me.

I remember in moments of utter despair thinking that the only way this would ever stop was to go back and beg for his forgiveness. I can't even believe I am saying that now but, in those moments, it felt like that would be the only way I could make it all stop.

Luckily because of that support I never ever gave into those feelings, and I am eternally grateful for that.

After a few months of living with my mother, I got my own house. I remember the day I moved into my new home as the day that gave me hope for the future. Not only was it the day I moved to a place of my own – a place I could feel safe and call home – but it was also the first time I had felt happy, calm and at peace, in forever.

I still remember the exact moment that it hit me: I was happy.

The French doors were open, my new partner was sitting on the top step leading down to the garden and I was in the kitchen. He shouted to me to come to him and, as I got to the door, I saw a pony from the field opposite, standing with its head practically over the gate just looking at us. What a welcome to my new home!

As I sat there on the steps, smiling away, I was suddenly aware of this feeling of peace throughout my entire body and, at that moment, I felt truly happy.

For the first time in I don't know how long, I was truly happy. The anxiety that normally coursed through my body was gone and was replaced with a feeling of peace. I can't describe how amazing that feeling was. It gave me such hope for the future, hope that at some point I could be in a place where I could feel this way all of the time.

I had lived with that intense anxiety for so long that it took a few moments to register that it wasn't there at all. That moment on the step not only gave me hope for the future, but also hope the anxiety I felt might one day disappear completely too.

Fast forward to now and it has pretty much gone. Yes, there are still occasions when I see him or think I see him that I can feel the overwhelming anxiety rise again, but thankfully it's short-lived and I now have the tools and strategies I need to be able to restore peace and calmness in my body.

When I first left, I was pretty excited for the future. I was thinking about how I could finally create the life I wanted. However, as things went on, the excitement faded, and I was really struggling to think about even having a life.

I remembered a conversation with a friend years earlier when I was going through my divorce. She told me how I was going to go on an emotional rollercoaster with no idea when it would end, so to help me get through it, I would need to find myself, to rediscover the things I enjoyed doing and what I wanted in my life moving forward.

I wasn't sure how exactly I was going to find myself or even what I enjoyed doing anymore, so started journaling, trying to remember who I was before any of this. I wrote lists of the things that I enjoyed doing, even going back to when I was a lot younger. One of the ways of finding myself was through reconnecting and spending time with old friends. I had always been quite a social person and I had missed having those friends in my life.

One of those friends was instrumental in supporting me after the break-up and the struggles that followed. We had been friends since we were teenagers, and he was someone I felt I could truly be myself around. He actively encouraged me to take control, to be strong and independent again. He challenged me to see myself differently and to see my worth.

For a long time, I felt very broken. I was living in fear, and I had all of this shit in my head about what I had been through. I felt so stupid because I hadn't seen the true level of abuse I had been experiencing. Everything I had believed about myself and my relationship I began to question, I felt utterly lost, I had no idea who I was or how to think for myself.

Through the love and support I received from him, I have been able to find my own way. He has allowed me to just be me, helping me most by allowing me the space to find myself. I am blessed that he has been there every step of the way, first as a friend and then as my partner. He has always been there when I needed him to be and, at the same time, he encouraged me to create a space for myself so I could regain my independence. I am so incredibly grateful to him for being alongside me on this journey.

In the early days when I felt like I was a complete mess, I was feeling so lost and really struggling to deal with everything. He used to take me mountain biking in the forest. I felt utterly useless, but he would keep telling me I could do it. Of course, I never believed him. Why would I? I hadn't experienced that kind of encouragement previously, in fact I'd had the complete opposite.

We'd ride through the forest – or often, in my case, walk my bike through the forest – to the trails. The voice of my ex would be so loud in my head, telling me I couldn't do it. "You can't get to the end of the street without stopping for a drink!"

I would be in tears struggling to quieten the voice of my ex, all the while Gary would be encouraging me that I could do it. He was so patient. On this particular day, I remember feeling like a kid as he stood there with his arms wide open ready to catch me as I tried to learn the trail step by step. The whole time I was battling with that voice in my head constantly telling me I couldn't do it.

His voice has been in my head so much. When it was at its worst it was like he still had his claws in me, they penetrated deep inside my mind, always influencing and manipulating my thoughts and behaviour. I couldn't escape them or switch them off.

I remember this one day when I was in my new house, I was standing washing dishes and then putting them on the draining board to dry. As I did this, I could hear his voice in my head, putting me down, about how when I lived in the home before we were together, he saw how I always left the dishes drying on the draining board. He used to make me feel like it was so bad of me to do that.

With his voice always there, it was like there was no escape from him. I had left him, and I was now in my own home, safe from him, but was I really? Because there he was in my head, still trying to control me and make me feel bad about myself.

I stood there feeling like I needed to dry them and put them away in the cupboard to shut him up and make me feel better. I made a choice there and then that I was in control, and I was not to give in and feel like he could still control me. Instead, I shut up his voice by saying, 'Fuck you, this is my house, I will do what I want to do!' And I left them there on the drainer to dry.

There have been so many times since that I have had to remind myself that he no longer controls my life, but I have battled with still hearing his voice in my head over the years. It is something I have had to consciously make an effort to separate in my mind, his voice and influence from my own thoughts and feelings.

Looking back to when we were together, and it feels strange to admit this, but I never really understood the extent of the abuse while I was in the relationship. I realised that it had become really toxic and that I was really unhappy, but I also believed I was nuts or a 'fruit loop' as I was so often called. If I'm honest with myself, I don't even think I was fully aware of the extent of the abuse until quite a while after I had left.

This has been something that has been a real struggle for me to get my head around. How stupid was I that I had not seen exactly what was happening? I have also tried to get to grips with what he did and how he did it.

When I was trying to explain to people what happened, it was so difficult because the manipulation and coercion was often so subtle. I couldn't get my head around it and I would be left questioning myself or playing it down.

It's totally bonkers to me that I really couldn't grasp how he did it and there are things that even now I still can't comprehend.

While we were together, I went for counselling a number of different times, and I saw a few different counsellors. I was having massive panic attacks, my anxiety was out of control and I really thought that I was mad. I am now able to see how I was made to believe there was something wrong with me and that the way I was feeling was me losing my mind.

When the counsellor I was seeing would help me to start seeing some of the flaws in the relationship, I would just stop going. Looking back, I didn't want to believe there was a problem in the relationship and I think part of the reason I went for counselling was that I wanted to learn ways in which I could be okay in the relationship as it was, how I could keep my shit together and be okay with how things were.

I felt like I was totally mad, I couldn't get control of my emotions and I was feeling this deep emotional pain. I felt so insecure, like I wasn't enough to make him happy.

So many times, I tried to pull it together, only to find myself time and time again falling apart, usually in a heap on the bathroom floor, as he stood by taunting me, asking if I was going to the bathroom to cry again.

I couldn't work out what the hell was wrong with me.

It has taken a long time to realise that there was nothing really wrong with me.

I don't know when I became aware of the full extent of

the abuse in the relationship. I can remember talking to the police, describing my experiences. I saw the looks on their faces as they told me those experiences weren't normal.

When I confided in friends trying to make sense of what had happened, they would say, 'You know that's not normal, though, don't you? That's abusive.' Honestly no, I don't know that I did. When I was with him, I wanted to believe the best about him. Even when I knew he was lying to me, a part of me absolutely wanted to believe him.

I remember the last counsellor I saw pointing out that I was showing him how to treat me. By the way I responded to him, I was telling him it was okay. I was telling him it was okay? I had lost all perspective of what was normal in a relationship, and I was angry at myself for being part of it and accepting it.

There are things that didn't become apparent when I was in the relationship. I believed I still had my independence and freedom. Although I always felt really strange about going out. It's hard to explain, but it was like I felt bad for leaving him alone and so would limit how long I was out.

A couple of my close friends were in a band, and I would have nights out to see them. On the odd occasion he came along, but I mostly went to see them alone. I would try to make the most of these nights alone with my friends, pretending everything was okay and trying to enjoy being me again.

In arguments, he would say how I was different when I had been out with my friends. I never quite understood what he meant until, in an argument after I left, he said that whenever I had been out with friends that I was always different, like 'I had had a taste of freedom'.

It didn't even register at that moment. It was months later when I began to see the significance of that comment. I wasn't ever really free. All that time I thought I was free to come and go as I pleased, but now I realised I wasn't.

The journey to rebuilding myself and my life has been quite a ride. I have gone from feeling like I am free, to I can't cope anymore and I need it to end, to feeling like I am finally living my life my way and I am happy. It felt like I was broken into tiny pieces, and I would have to rebuild my life and my sense of self one piece at a time.

The beginning of the journey was hard, and I really didn't want to deal with it. Getting through it involved a lot of chocolate, a bit of alcohol and a whole lot of avoidance. All I wanted to do was numb the thoughts, drown out his voice, reduce the anxiety and hope it would eventually go away.

Thankfully, I quite quickly realised that was a rubbish coping strategy and I needed to try other things to help me get through this. I started to go back to counselling, as I really needed a space where I could talk openly about what was happening and how I was feeling without any fear of judgement or upsetting people. Talking to someone who was completely detached from the situation was so important. I had so much going on inside me, I needed to be able to make sense of it.

Another way that I was able to do this was through journaling. It's something that I have done for as long as I can remember. Even in the relationship I used to do it to try to understand why I was feeling the way I did. When my thoughts had been racing all over the place, journaling really helped me to slow them down, make sense of them and see what I could do to help me in that moment.

Being a coach and hypnotherapist and having worked in mental health for twenty years, I had been lucky enough to be connected with a huge network of different therapists and healers. Over the last few years, I have undergone a number of different talking and alternative therapies to help me process and heal from my experiences.

I have learned how to tune into and listen to myself and my body to help me to discover blocks, to break through them and get past them. This is a continuous journey of re-finding myself, it feels like I uncover small parts of myself pretty much daily. The more I have become aware of myself, the more I am able to learn how to accept myself.

That process of separating what is your belief, thought, feeling, behaviour from what you have taken on from someone else takes time. As I started to remember who I was, I looked at myself in the mirror and didn't fully recognise myself. Who I thought would be looking back at me wasn't who I saw.

Even my wardrobe was full of clothes that weren't me anymore. I had changed everything about me to please him, convincing myself it would make me more attractive or more lovable or just make me feel like I was enough for him. He would love me and be kind to me if I just did everything he wanted.

I needed to learn to love myself for who I am, to feel like I am enough, independent of anyone else. This is still a work in progress, and I know I still have a way to go before I can love and accept myself fully and completely.

The use of hypnotherapy recording, meditations and affirmations has really helped me with this as they help me to rewrite the story I have been telling myself for so long. I feel much more connected to myself, and I am always learning new ways to heal and feel my way through the pain.

I look back at just how far I have come, and I am incredibly proud of how much I have grown and all that I have achieved. I have completely changed my life and done things I never thought I would. With the love and support from my partner, family and friends, I have done things I never imagined I could.

For over ten years I had been running my coaching business as a bit of a hobby alongside my full-time job and, in 2018, I joined a coaching programme that changed my perspective on how I could potentially grow my business and earn a living doing what I loved.

I started on this completely new journey where I was now taking on clients across the world. It was beyond my wildest dreams; I could never have believed this would be possible. I truly believe it would never have happened if I hadn't got out of that relationship. I would never have had the confidence or self-belief to even pursue the opportunity.

With this newfound confidence and self-belief and a lot of support from my partner, I took the biggest step of all and in December 2019 I left my career of twenty years to go all-in on growing my coaching business. Over the years I had come to really hate it there and it was beginning to have a massive impact on my own mental health. I had never before felt like I had a way out, but everything was different now, I was stronger, more confident and I had all the support I needed to walk away from it. I could see how important it was to walk away from things that weren't good for me in order to create a better life.

Through my coaching I feel like I have found my life purpose and I am now able to create a life for myself and my family that I love.

I would dream about what I wanted my business to look like. I wanted to work with international clients, travelling the world to work with them in person. I was absolutely blown away when this became a reality. In March 2020 I flew out to Spain for one week to work in person with my client.

How could this be my life, my job?

I had made this happen, the choices I had made, the things I had been through and the support I had around me had got me to this point in my life. I was finally living my dream life and it felt so good.

Not only has my journey allowed me to grow in strength and confidence, but it has also allowed me to help my clients deal with their issues in a deeper way and create even more impact in their lives.

When I had the idea that I didn't want to reach forty and still be living that same life, I never thought for one second that I would be able to change my life in the way I have.

Looking back, I thought I could just end the relationship, walk away and get on with my life. However, I massively underestimated the healing that would have to take place and the journey I would have to go on to find myself again.

I'm not going to lie, it hasn't all been rosy. I have had to experience the pain and feel my way through it to find a place of healing. I have faced incredibly tough times where I have felt lost and stuck, and I have had to dig deep to find the strength to keep moving forward.

As I continue to find my way, I can wholeheartedly say that all that I have been through on my journey has been worth it to reach the place I am at now.

I have so much hope and excitement for what the future has in store.

I am Donna, this is my truth, I own who I am and every part of the journey I have been on to get here.

Use this space to journal:

Journal questions:

1. Can you identify some thoughts in your head that are actually from your ex?
2. Acknowledge that these thoughts are not yours. You are now able to consciously choose what to think instead. Decide what you want to think and rewrite them with your own truth.

_____

_____

_____

_____

_____

_____

_____

_____

_____

_____

_____

_____

_____

I Am the Sum of My Experiences

Sandie Davis

L et me tell you what life was like in England in the 1970s.

It was a creative and exciting time and, for a music fan, there were so many icons. My first love was David Bowie and glam rock; I was captivated by Peter Gabriel and prog rock; then came punk rock and it was deliciously dangerous to listen to the Sex Pistols.

British TV had cuddly programmes like *All Creatures Great and Small* and *Coronation Street*, there was hints of subversive broadcasting with *Monty Python's Flying Circus* and escapism in *Doctor Who*, but there was also the 'cheeky' comedy of Benny Hill that was massively popular.

But what was everyday life like for women in the 1970s?

After the 'swinging sixties' and the rise of feminism, change was in the air but hadn't reached daily life for ordinary women. Most women held traditional homemaker roles, bringing up children and having a meal on the table for the husband returning from work. Many women had limited access to contraception and gender roles were still very clear cut.

Increasingly, women were in the workplace, but they tended to hold part-time underpaid jobs. Women did not have equal pay with similar roles held by men and for the woman who entered a male-dominated profession, the glass ceiling was made out of strong safety glass to protect the men above it from stroppy females. Women who tried to break through faced challenging situations and limited success.

Unbelievably, in the early 70s, a woman could not take out a credit card or sign a loan agreement without the authority of her father or her husband, bank accounts were in the name of her spouse or sometimes in both names, and taking out an account for a single woman often needed a man's guarantee. Women were seen as a financial risk and widows or single women had to fight for financial independence.

Women were underrepresented in government, a fraction of women attended university, access to professional jobs was restricted; men very much held the power in all aspects of life.

The law did not look kindly on women; rape within marriage was not a crime and elderly male judges accepted that what happened in the marital house was the responsibility of the husband. Domestic violence was difficult to prove and not generally challenged.

Abortion had only just become law in certain cases but was still challenged and held stigma; women were victims of their own reproductive cycle and the control over that was held by law makers.

So, how is 1970s social commentary in a book meant to encourage and inspire women now? I wanted to set the scene for what is to come in my story. It sets the scene for why I had unhealthy relationships and why I understood these to be acceptable; it gives some background to the decisions I made and introduces the idea that we do not always have the freedom of choice we think we have.

Often, we berate ourselves for bad decisions we have made, particularly in our relationships. It is still commonplace for a woman in an abusive situation to be blamed and blame herself for the abuse she and her family are experiencing. We tell each other it is NOT YOUR FAULT but still this unconscious attitude sometimes prevails. We need to recognise and challenge this.

I look back at the seventies, when I was a teenager, and further back in time and I have come to the realisation that much of our decision making is not actually freedom of choice. We have grown up within a culture so governed by the patriarchal system that our decisions have actually been made for us hundreds of years ago by men in power and we are conditioned by unequal social structures to think that we have choice.

Not only that but we are conditioned to take the blame when we are treated badly. I remember clearly a song as I was growing up, 'Young Girl" by Gary Puckett and the Union Gap. I identified so much with this as it tells the tale of a younger girl in a relationship with an older man; what became my reality!

What I now realise when reading the lyrics is that

the blame is firmly placed with the girl and not the responsibility of the older, supposedly mature man. The lyrics place all the responsibility with the girl and state she is the reason the relationship existed. Meanwhile he claims no responsibility for his actions as the older man. It only dawned on me as an adult how the young girl takes the blame for any indiscretions, certainly not the adult man!

Some women are unable to spot when they are in an abusive or domineering relationship; some women find feminism intimidating and unnecessary; our place in our culture is so ingrained, it is invisible but very real. The patriarchy is alive and well and thriving even now.

Next time you find yourself taking the blame for a poor decision you have made, be gentle with yourself, many of us have made life decisions with the weight of history and culture that is not on our side. When we eventually make that decision that is solely for our own benefit, it is made difficult for us, but it is very definitely worth pursuing!

So, back to me in the seventies, growing up and discovering relationships. I was a quiet child and quite solitary. I was brought up with my mum and nana, so had no male family members to build relationships with. Predictably, this made me naïve, but I was blissfully unaware of that! I had a great imagination and early experiences with boys were purely in my head, in amongst being a singer in a rock band or an actor in *Star Trek* – I remember crayoning a whole console of spaceship buttons on a chest of drawers and happily sitting alongside an imaginary Mr Spock for many happy hours.

It was wonderful to be brought up in a secure female home with strong women. My grandfather, my only male relative, died when I was a toddler. I know our family must have struggled financially, but again I had little awareness of this. I was brought up in an environment where women made decisions and maybe this meant I was ill equipped for the real world. My mum worked full time, I saw this as the norm and had aspirations to have a career in journalism.

At school I was popular, my friendship group had a lot of boys in it, which I am sure was misconstrued, but apart from my first – and pretty much my only – teenage boyfriend, these were my friends.

Outwardly, I was confident and outgoing, but I was still pretty insecure; I blushed easily and there was one teacher at school who delighted in saying 'hello gorgeous' each time he saw me in the corridor or even in a lesson just to see me blush and be totally embarrassed and uncomfortable. Nobody challenged this to my knowledge – was this abusive? It certainly wasn't acceptable. I was kissed by a couple of teachers. I thought I was special, it never occurred to me that it wasn't acceptable – I was fair game for men and my outward blossoming sexuality was okay to be shared.

At this time, it was seen as acceptable for some men to be able to attempt to kiss or grope any woman they took a liking to, and if it was a younger woman they could exert power over all the better. I must stress, I know that not all men are like this, and we should be careful not to tag all men as predators. I just know from my experience that this happened, and you need only look at the number of high-profile men that have been convicted of historic abuse that it was not just my experience and, in those times, things were acceptable that are not now.

It has only been relatively recently that I have looked back with more awareness and see that I was on a path to negative relationships. My decisions were influenced from an early age and I did not develop the confidence to manage or direct my relationships for my benefit.

All this was such a long time ago; or not that long ago at all.

An altogether different time; or maybe not.

I was fifteen when I met a guy who was older and exciting, he was knowledgeable and worldly and I felt very grown up being with him – he was twenty-eight. At the time, I had no concept of the power imbalance in this relationship and never wondered what on earth he was doing dating a schoolgirl – so very naïve!

He helped me restyle my hair and buy new clothes – to turn me into a woman, I thought. He took my virginity in a transit van on the side of the A6 – even then I did not see this as an abusive relationship or some sort of grooming, I felt grown up and very special. Even now the thing I am most angry about is that he manipulated me into asking my nana for money to pay his debts. I feel stupid writing this and I have to actively remind myself it was NOT my fault.

There are still older men, richer men, who pursue having a young woman as a prize, as a possession – this is not the place to explore that, but if you have been influenced by someone with more power than you then you have the right to know you are the better person and you are in a much more healthy place now.

Unfortunately for him, I also have a short attention span and, although I was with him a fairly long time, when I was seventeen, I met a local guy nearer my age – only a bit nearer, he was still twenty-four!

There is something here about the old cliché of me looking for a father figure. I have heard lots of theories about having a family member dying early and the effect this has on self-image and self-blame. I have read about women who search for a missing father figure and how fathers are important – maybe, just maybe, this is another theory perpetuated by our culture that may not be as influential as we think. I think boys my age scared me a little, although the real threat came from the older, more predatory man.

At this time, I had left college before gaining my qualifications and was working in a local town centre pub. I loved this time and had loads of fun and positive experiences that went with pub culture then. This was a busy market pub with a thriving lunchtime trade, and I learned how to carry five plates of food to a table at once – I did try to achieve seven, but never managed it. In the evenings, the customers changed to groups of guys out on the town, and I became a really very good pool player, beating most of them regularly. I was on the pub pool team and when we played away at other pubs, having a girl on the team was shocking!

My new relationship seemed conventional enough and was leading towards buying a house – his money, his name on the deeds, his decision – but then this became a more classic abusive relationship when he started slapping me when I irritated him and his desire to have risky sexual experiences in public places. I know now that this was about humiliating me and displaying his ownership of me. Neither of us would have been able to define this at the time – it is just how it was. I think I knew I had to escape this relationship but ending it was out of the question for me. I was understandably sad when I found he was sleeping with other women, but it allowed me to back off from the relationship. It seemed really fortunate that a lunchtime regular in the pub started to show an interest in me.

I was nineteen when I met the man I married. He had already taken a job offer 200 miles away from my hometown, so of course I went with him to live in a town where I knew literally no one at the age of twenty.

Thinking back, I can't even remember discussing it with my nana. I probably just upped and left. I was young, insensitive, totally obsessed with the man I was with. I was not able to see the pain this might have caused others by not having self-awareness or, as I now know, any sense of self-worth. My whole sense of self was wound up in the man I was seeing at the time. My mum had married by this time and had moved away, and I just disregarded any feelings they may have had so I could be with him.

I was married for years, I was well provided for, I had three amazing, beautiful children, I lived in an impressive house, I went to a range of corporate events and dinners, I was not physically abused, I could stay at home and bring up my children and have the benefits of a financially comfortable marriage. At this time, the definition of an abusive relationship was very much based on beatings and physical abuse. I had been in a relationship where I felt unsafe, and my marriage did not feel abusive based on my knowledge at the time. It felt safe not to have to make financial decisions or be worried about pensions. I was unaware of the cost of the mortgage and utilities and school fees. I had housekeeping that I used to buy our groceries and other things for the children. All very normal and safe.

We moved house again and became friendly with two other couples across the road from us. I was still so naïve and inexperienced, I accepted without question the way our marriage was. I never had a parental marriage to compare it to, I did not have close friends to compare anything with, I didn't know enough about myself to be an effective parent; I never questioned my reality.

My life was fairly unremarkable, but it was livened up massively by my new friends. We shared meals, lovely long summer afternoons with our small children and lots of Beaujolais Nouveau. These were proper grown-up women with opinions and careers, and they had a huge influence on how I began to see my marriage and myself. We had long conversations about politics and relationships, I found I enjoyed listening to different viewpoints, reflecting on ideas and learning to disagree and formulate my own opinions. I think I became aware of my personal intellectual capability, and I quite liked it!

I missed them terribly when we moved another sixty miles away after my husband gained a new job; I may not have had daily contact with them, but their influence stayed with me. I started to volunteer with a local youth work organisation, and I related well to the young people I worked with, probably because I hadn't properly grown up myself. I was fostering a sense of self-worth and developing an outside interest.

My husband started his own business and I started to take on admin tasks to support this, discovering I could do that as well. I was learning new skills and finding career opportunities that had been lost for decades. I learned to type; ironically, I didn't do this at school when being a typist was something girls could do, but I did this late and now in the world we live in where the keyboard is so vital to everything we do, I am grateful I learned to type with more than one finger. I took my first accredited course since leaving college and gained an NVQ3 in administration. I was so proud of that certificate, and I still get a thrill from gaining external validation of my skills – I do like a certificate!

I thought it was supportive when my husband offered to house the organisation I was volunteering with in his offices and provide services for us; maybe in reflection it kept me close to keep an eye on me. I became more unsettled and felt more stifled, it was almost like being a teenager who has grown out of the family house and needs to leave the nest to stretch their wings. I married young and I remember thinking that I had been in the relationship almost twenty years and, if nothing changed, I would have another twenty or thirty or even forty years ahead of me. I couldn't see a way it might change, and this prospect scared me more than the end of the relationship did.

This need to stretch my wings led to the end of the marriage. I take responsibility for my actions that led to the marriage ending, and I am not proud of that time in my life at all. I knew it had to end and it ended the only way I could see out. It is true that we should learn from every experience – good or bad. It is also true we need to find a way to be kind to ourselves and, if needed, forgive ourselves in order to move on.

I put the youth work volunteering on hold and got a part-time admin job to start to build some sort of financial independence. I started to think about pensions and all sorts of grown-up things I had never had to consider. This was daunting but every time I understood something new, I felt more empowered to have a say in the direction my life was taking. I began to feel I could actually be in charge of my own destiny.

My new role was in the local hospital and was really interesting, although I came across a new type of person I hadn't been aware of – the hospital consultant. Their word was law, they made daily decisions about life and death, they had vast knowledge, they were treated like gods and they were so important! I was immediately intimidated and didn't want to spend all day with people who disregarded my value and contribution. I started to want to return to working with young people who maybe needed me more than the consultants and where I could be more useful. I wanted to be doing something of value. I was discovering a sense of vocation and wanted to have a profession and not just skim through life with no depth.

I had to learn to be an independent person. I was brought up not having awareness about money, even though it was tight, and my adult life so far had not had money worries. I had never talked or learnt about money or had financial independence. I had never lived alone before, I had never been the 'responsible adult'. This wasn't an easy transition, but I learnt and I developed and we can achieve things we never thought were possible if we are brave and give ourselves a chance to. Practical changes often run alongside emotional changes and managing them all is tricky.

Obviously, the lovely house had to go and having to dispose of a large amount of furniture and stuff was a challenge – my daughter's first car caught fire the week before we moved and I had to explain to the new owners that the wreck of a car would move soon! Sometimes we have to go through chaotic times to come out the other side. I rented a gingerbread cottage for us to live in. Okay, so it wasn't actually gingerbread, but it had similarities, like the tiny mice that ran through the lounge and the really strange plumbing.

I do have positive memories of living there. I think I was able to build an adult relationship with my daughter and we bonded so much in that house. She was a grown woman herself – even though she once phoned me at work after she went for a walk and got lost! The materialistic things had been taken away but we talked more and made happy memories. We did not have the lifestyle we left but we shared good times. I have always loved football and we watched England matches together as I explained the rules – and how to deal with the despair when they lost! But we were silly and laughed together lots. I bought her a Tweety Pie fishing rod (I repeat, she was an adult, but this summed up our days together). She managed to get it caught in the neighbour's tree and we had to go round and ask for our fishing rod back.

Even though we had none of the conventional benefits and luxuries of the family home, we had happy times and a lot of that was because we were finding ourselves and choosing to be happy. It is true that money in itself does not bring happiness and joy can be found in circumstance irrespective of the monthly income.

Through work I built a completely different friendship group with people who related to me as an individual and not my place in a couple. These friendships were more diverse and actually more anarchic, and I further developed my individual values and attitudes and sense of self.

So, not long after turning forty, I found a job in youth work where they sent me to university to gain a qualification to allow me to develop a career in the sector. Over the three years I spent studying and working I gained a huge insight into my own issues and life as well as behavioural theory. All my assignments became cathartic as I explored motivations, relationships and social constructs. I began to understand more about the impact on my life of external factors. There have been two places I have learnt so much – studying at university and working in the pub!

I was able to work full time and earn the salary that came with that, I was able to focus on something for me that I was good at and that I enjoyed doing and that was useful. I developed my career and took on a role training other adults to be youth workers. I found a love for developing people and seeing those light-bulb moments of realisation when people discover something new that will stay with them on their journey. I found that as I trained and developed my career, my salary rose! Who knew! You don't have to start at the bottom of the ladder at age eighteen, you can start at any time and, even at age forty, we still have up to thirty years of a working life to go – you are never as old as you think you are, there is still so much life to have. When I was a teenager, forty seemed ancient – when you reach it, it's not so bad!

I found myself in a place where being self-sufficient was feasible. I found identity in my working life and was accepted for myself not as one half of a couple. I was earning my own money and had a bank account. I will say that financial independence has been a rocky road. I have made poor financial decisions and still mess up sometimes. I still have a flawed relationship with money, but it is getting better.

My first big purchase after independence was a car and I made such a really bad decision with that – I chose a car because it was red and had a soft top, I didn't notice the dreadful condition it was in or the smile of the guy selling it when I didn't even haggle the price. I realised what a bad decision it was when driving on a motorway with my daughter and she had to hold the roof in place from her seat to stop it blowing off completely. It leaked dreadfully and the first MOT was a pricey affair. Accept you will make poor decisions, but bounce back, don't dwell on it, keep on going on the new path you are making, just learn from it and next time buy the sensible car!

So, where am I now? I have married again, on completely different terms. I feel an equal partner, I still have financial independence, I do not want to give up my hard-won gains and thankfully my partner understands that. We discuss and exchange views, we share interests, but we also have individual passions that we follow independently. We enjoy being together but can spend time apart; it's a positive relationship. I think it is important to learn that not all relationships are the same and we don't have to be fearful of losing something of ourself if we commit to a new one; we don't have to stay single for the rest of our lives – unless, of course, we choose to!

I am in a more positive relationship, and this seems to permeate other relationships in my life. I get on so well with my new wider family; my relationship with my previous in-laws was frightful. I think I am more able to value friendships and family ties, but I am also comfortable in my own skin much more and can spend time with myself.

I value working and have been fortunate to develop a career in a sector I am passionate about and enjoy. Yes, I do still work because it is financially necessary, but I gain personal self-worth from it as well and it still makes me feel good about myself. It might not be work that brings that for everyone, it is good to seek out what fulfils you and brings that joy.

I do still have issues! I am not the perfect, rounded human I seem to be describing; I am dreadful at making decisions and would rather go along with someone else's decision about all things big and small. I have started to make a conscious effort to try to make decisions about small things, like what to watch on TV, and I believe I need to exercise my decision-making capability so I get better at it; it does still feel uncomfortable, though.

I also have a deep-seated need to keep things to myself and not share – am I less trusting still? I will be aware of events happening but will only share them at the last minute, I don't share my personal views easily and I keep different parts of my life in little compartments, it feels safer that way.

It takes a long time to recover from negative experiences and recovery can only happen if you address the fallout – I have chosen for a long time to be content and not open the can of worms that probably still remains, but it is so well sealed that I still prefer it that way! Writing this has been as cathartic as I intend to be, thank you very much!

It is worth accepting that growth and recovery are long-term activities. Don't expect the world to suddenly click into place as soon as you choose a life change. But be encouraged, every day it gets a tiny bit better and, as you look back, you can see just how very far you have come, under your own strength, with your own choices. For example, I have so many phobias and fears that I am only just now addressing: fear of heights, fear of flying, fear of boats, fear of the dark, fear of the dentist, fear of spiders (although that is just common sense!). In the past couple of years, I have started to challenge those fears and explore why I seem to be so fearful – I don't want to be governed by irrational fears anymore.

As I have got older, I seem to have developed a nurturing persona. I have had a number of job roles where I have formed great working relationships with younger colleagues, and I seem to have fallen into a maternal role with lots of people. I think all experiences can be turned into positive influences in your life; horrible experiences can make you into the best listener and people instinctively know you understand. I feel more at peace with myself at sixty than at any time before, it really is never too late to make choices to improve yourself and your life. We are always growing, always learning. I may have lost many years in a state of acceptance and obliviousness, but I'm living my best life now. Change is scary but not scary at the same time – it can bring new experiences and opportunities.

As I have become a grandparent (just the best experience ever) I seem to have taken on that role at work as well! In my present job I am known as Nana Sandie, and I revel in that. I am nana to my grandchildren but also to a range of fur babies who love nana for the treats she carries around with her! I may have made mistakes in the past, but I am the best nana ever and I finally have a role I can be confident in. I still want to be a rock star or actor, but I'm more accepting that this may not happen!

I refuse to be defined by my past and I think that any disruption caused by dwelling on the past is not worth it. I am happy, I have independence, I am the sum of my experiences, I am Nana Sandie!

Use this space to journal:

Journal questions:

1. Are you hanging on to guilt for what you think are bad decisions?
2. Can you see any external circumstances that influenced those?
3. Can you finally forgive yourself for those decisions?
4. Remember you are brave, you are doing the right thing, you are awesome.

_____

_____

_____

_____

_____

_____

_____

_____

_____

_____

_____

_____

_____

_____

Stepping into My Designed Life

Victoria Padmore

I have several stories about leaving abusive relationships. I could probably think back to each one and explain how I found the strength to leave, I could tell you the breaking point that made me realise I absolutely had to leave, and I could tell you about the celebration and support I got to leave these relationships. However, this is all useless information because I can also tell you that it never lasted long. I would either decide to give him another chance or, more commonly, I would move on to another relationship. These new relationships would quickly erode into abuse in one form or another. I was in a cycle of abusive relationships and so very confused about how I kept finding myself with men who promised me they were different only to show me they were exactly the same. Those stories are about how I left but not about how I built an incredible life away from abuse because I never seemed to be able to get to that point. I always seemed to be able to do what others perceived as the difficult bit, actually leaving, but not the real hard work of staying away and rebuilding myself and my life.

I moved from man to man and the abuse just escalated in each of them, with the last man I was in a relationship with adding physical abuse, a world I had never really experienced before. I had found myself in a world of violence where "getting a slap" from your partner was expected from time to time and victim shaming was prevalent. When I tried to reach out for help, "Why didn't you give him a slap back?" was something I heard regularly from the circles he had dragged me into.

Let me just take a moment here to say any physical altercation within a relationship towards anyone in that relationship is not normal and is never excusable!

I now know how I got into this cycle of abusive relationships. Quite simply, I had no direction in life. I had my career goals and amazingly throughout all of this I was still achieving these goals, but I had no direction in my personal life. I saw all my value within my career. I didn't actually know what I wanted out of life. At the end of each relationship, I was so scared of the unknown. Once the drama of the break-ups had settled, I would get severe anxiety of "what now?!" I had no idea what my life would look like moving forward. For each of these relationships, I had focused so much on what he wanted and how to keep him happy that when that focus was taken away, I was simply lost. I had built my identity so much around the man I was with that I did not know what I wanted when I wasn't ensuring he got what he wanted.

I now realise that this led me to search for answers and a direction in life without knowing what I was actually searching for. In my search for answers, I attracted a certain type of man, one that was more than happy to tell me what I wanted in life. Manipulative men had a blank canvas to paint on as I had completely lost my own identity over the years, I had no wants or desires. I would swing from wanting marriage to saying "its just a piece of paper" or wanting several children to not even wanting one. All these opinions were simply a mirror of the life he wanted.

In my last relationship, violence, drugs, court cases and prison visits all became part of my life because they were part of his. Initially, I desperately wanted to save him from all these horrors, but instead – in trying to save him – I was dragged into it further myself. This made his hold on me even tighter. I was in his world now and I didn't know how to survive in it without him.

Life became a game of survival, looking to the future was not an option. I actively avoided thinking of the future because then I would have to admit that things would never change if I stayed in this relationship. I would have to admit that I was never going to "save him" because he simply didn't want saving. When in the relationship, I did not have the capability to dream and design a better future for myself because I would have to admit that he did not fit into those dreams at all and that was something I just wasn't ready to hear. So, I continued for years, just focusing on surviving that day and falling into bed at night, emotionally and physically exhausted, not even thinking of what the next day would hold. I was living in a world where fighting through the day was the only focus for most people, even tomorrow wasn't a focus. This meant months became years without lifting up my head to look around and find an out.

So, what changed? I now have a beautiful marriage with two amazing children. I am safe, I am loved, I am valued and, more importantly, I love and value myself! We plan for the future and our plans are so very exciting to me. It wasn't a quick, easy process to get here and at the time I didn't really realise all the work I was putting in to get to where I am now. However, I am now able to look back on this journey and explain exactly how I created an incredible life away from abuse.

The last split was forced upon me by Her Majesty's Prison Service. A split that truly broke my heart at the time. However, what it delivered was a time in my life where I had space to breathe without looking for a new relationship. I was officially still in a relationship but without his overwhelming presence daily. I was able to lift my head up and truly look around without the fear and oppression I felt when he was home.

Without him around, I started to actually see the life I was living through my own eyes and what my future held if this continued. I stopped simply being a mirror of his wants, as he wasn't there to reflect from. I was forced to think of what I truly wanted in life, no one was there to tell me what I wanted anymore. Yes, this was scary to begin with, but it soon became so very freeing. It had to become about me again for the first time in many years. The concept of putting my feelings, wants and desires first had become alien to me, and it took time to remember how to do this again.

I had finally lifted my head and looked around, to see things for myself. Have you ever looked at an optical illusion picture where the same picture is actually two different things?

This is a young woman looking away but also an old lady side on. Your mind will always see one of the women first and to you it is absolutely her in the picture, until someone points out the other woman hidden in there. All of a sudden, you lose the original image you saw and all you can see is the woman they saw first and have shown you. This is how I was viewing life, through someone else's eyes. I was horrified at the drugs and violence when I first saw them but once I saw them through others' eyes, as a normal part of everyday life, I seemed to fall in line with their view and their reality. I needed to stop listening to what others told me to see and be true to myself about what this world looked liked through my own eyes. So, this is where I started to rewrite my life. I had to start by cleaning the canvas before I could design a beautiful future to work towards.

I remember when I was a lot younger and just starting out dating. My older brother tried to give me a piece of advice:

"If you don't see him as your husband, then why continue to date him?"

At the time, this felt so very heavy to me! I was just starting out dating and I was absolutely loving it, of course I wasn't thinking about marriage. I was having such fun getting to know all about dating and also getting to know more about myself. At that age, I had no idea what I wanted in a husband. Now, however, I see the absolute gold in this advice. It wasn't about seeing my date as my husband on first meeting him. It wasn't even about knowing what I did want in a husband. The advice was to be able to identify what I absolutely, definitely didn't want in my life and identify it quickly.

It is much easier to list what you absolutely don't want

in a relationship than what you do want. Looking back, had I taken his advice I would know that addiction, violence and prison were elements I did not want included in my life. So, when I met my boyfriend and saw his world included all of this should I have continued to date him? No, absolutely not.

It would take me many years to know what I did want in my life partner, but even at that young age I could have listed out what I definitely didn't want. It was in my naivety that I didn't even think these would ever be things that would even touch my world, let alone engulf it.

This, I now know, is all about setting boundaries and having the self-respect to uphold them. At this point in my life, having had a taste of all these things, I had to then set a new standard of boundaries. This was so much harder than setting them right from the beginning of my dating life. Putting this new set of boundaries in felt almost hypocritical to me. I had accepted so much from a partner and also partook myself so much in this world that how could I now stand up and say I no longer accepted these elements in my life?

So, step one had to be forgiveness. Full absolute forgiveness for my actions but mainly how I had treated myself. I had to drop the shame I felt, and the shame others had put on me, for allowing drugs and violence to become part of my daily life. I had to stand tall against all other opinions and say, "I deserve better!" I wiped that canvas clean. Just because I had accepted infidelity as part of my life before did not mean I had to accept it again; just because I had accepted violence as part of my life before did not mean I had to accept it again. The same went for verbal abuse, psychological abuse, financial abuse, it all had to become unacceptable. Boundaries can move, they are not predetermined by anything you have experienced in your life or from what you have accepted previously.

I felt liberated! I felt strong and I knew I would not accept these horrors to cast shade on my life ever again. Then the old anxiety kicked in and the question that had led to so many bad decisions previously screamed in my head, "What now?!"

I had identified what I didn't want in my life but had no idea what that left. I had cleaned the canvas but now the emptiness and nothingness this left was overwhelming. Previously I would go searching for the answer to this question externally. I would go looking for someone, anyone who could tell me what I wanted for my life and my future, obviously with awful consequences. The difference this time was that instead of looking externally for the answer to "what now?" I looked internally. I knew I had to find the answers within myself if I was to ever design that life I wanted to live and not a version of someone else's life.

The real shift came about when I started to actually get excited by what I wanted out of life and, more importantly, believing I deserved to be that happy! Now that I had cleaned the canvas, I could start painting a life I truly wanted to live. The blanks canvas became enticing, daring me to fill it with what I honestly wanted. I knew that to fight through this transitional stage of my life and become someone completely different, I needed to be excited about the possibilities on the other side of the journey. When faced with difficult changes in life, it is so important to know what awaits you on the other side, otherwise it is too easy to quit and revert back to what you know, no matter how miserable that made you.

So, I started designing an image. As a child, I had always been a dreamer, I was always good at imagining things in great detail. This is something I had lost as an adult, it felt silly and childish to dream of a different life. I now know this skill as visualisation, and it has become a tool I have used over and over when I wanted to step to a new chapter in my life. The image of the life I wanted to live was painted in minute detail and also to the extreme, and why not?! Why couldn't I dream big, why shouldn't I have outrageous goals to work towards? This was the biggest step in changing my life, not any actual physical actions but a change in mindset.

My mindset shifted from looking down and surviving to looking up and to the future and what I could create. I also needed to attach feelings to these images, so for me a list of wants just wasn't going to feel real enough. I could list that I wanted to be married, with children, a group of friends who supported me, a large house, my own business, a fabulous 4x4 car, etc., etc., etc., but that list would not excite me. That list could be anyone's list and did not hold emotional attachment for me. I had to paint these elements into an image of what my day would look like. Visualisation is more about feeling the results rather than listing them. I started to create visualisations of how my life would actually be if I created this life away from abuse; I actually visualised days.

I remember my first ever visualisation and I have kept this in my mind and my heart and still use it from time to time to reconnect with the direction I want for my life, and now to also celebrate how much of this visualisation I have already achieved.

My visualisation started where I was driving home from a fabulous lunch with a circle of amazing women who hold each other up and have me laughing from the moment I arrive till the moment I leave. I am driving a badass 4x4 car singing at the top of my voice to Beyonce, of course! I already connect to this as carefree, stress-free living. I am celebrating the feeling of having a group of friends who love and cherish each other. As I visualised this, I used to feel calmer and stronger, I could feel my shoulders loosen and my jaw unclench.

As I arrived home, I created an image of a dream house for me, a big winding driveway, beautiful front garden, statuesque double front doors, all mine. This gave me the feeling of success, of reward for hard work, of stability. I can tell you what the windows look like, what the house looks like when I open the doors, even what the flowers smell like!

Then I open the door and my husband shouts hello from the kitchen. Yes, he's handsome AND a great cook! I told you my visualisation was giving me the extremes! My cute puppy runs to meet me at the front door. I immediately feel welcome and safe and truly loved and appreciated.

As I walk through to the kitchen and its huge windows looking out into the garden, I see my children playing in our garden. My husband and I take a moment to stand and watch them for a while, hearts bursting with pride.

So, as the list said, I wanted to be married, with children, a group of friends who supported me, a large house, my own business, a fabulous 4x4 car, but what the visualisation gave me was feeling carefree, stress-free, successful, stable, loved, appreciated, proud. All those feelings felt worth fighting for far more than a list of material wants.

I built this visualisation when I had absolutely none of that and, yes, it felt like a different world, but my desire to have those feelings became so very strong for me. I created that visualisation sitting in a flat with holes punched in the walls and doors, tin foil still stuffed down the side of my sofa from his drug use, while I was still calling the prison to try and book visitation with my boyfriend, awaiting letters from him each week, a broken woman who had for years not felt any of those emotions. I created my biggest visualisations when I was at my lowest point because, at this point, I needed something outrageously extravagant so it was worth the painful journey of change I knew I was about to face. I had to believe that there was better out there and a life away from abuse could bring all this to me and more.

I would need that visualisation and the emotions that it held to move house, to stop the prison visits and ask for no more letters, to stand strong when I was hated and shamed for not supporting him anymore and when I was painted as the evil, heartless one. I needed to know and feel what I was working towards and why it would be worth it.

Once I had this vision of what I actually, genuinely wanted, I owed it to myself to make this happen. It couldn't just become an escapism. I did not want to just use it as my happy place to sit and imagine when I was having a tough day. It could not become my way to disengage with reality, I still needed to be very present in life. I didn't live there yet, so staying there all day would get me nowhere near it becoming reality. Once I believed I could create all those emotions in my daily life, I needed to take action to make it happen, not just imagine them. I knew that to move forward, every single life decision I made from that day onwards had to be a piece of the path that led to me having this life I designed.

So, my brother's advice came to mind at this point in my life. It was probably about eleven or twelve years after he gave it to me. I hadn't even thought of it since he said it but now, finally, I understood it. If I did not want something or someone in my life long-term, I shouldn't entertain it at all. I took this dating advice and made it a rule in all aspects of my life. I had my end goal and the feelings attached to that. If something or someone wanted to enter my life that I did not see fitting into that end goal, then I needed to question the relevance in my life. It is exactly that: MY life to live and I had to be responsible for everything I let into it. I guess it is like a diet, you have to make a decision whether the end goal of better fitness and a better body is worth giving up the daily cake and chocolate.

Is the short-term high of the calorie-filled food worth not reaching your end goal of better fitness and a better body?

When I was finally ready to get back to dating, I questioned, "Does he fit into my visualisation of coming home to him in our fabulous house, caring for me and our children?" If the answer was obviously no then continuing a relationship with him took me on a different life path that didn't lead to the life I truly wanted to live. I applied this to other life decisions too, career decisions, who I connected to as friends, even family. It became my compass for all life decisions, and it hasn't steered me wrong yet. It hasn't been a straight path and I haven't been perfect. I've had moments of metaphorically stuffing my face with cake and chocolate, especially in the early days, but it became less and less the more I started to feel these new emotions and realise how worth it this new life was.

In my last abusive relationship, wanting more for myself always held such guilt over who I would have to leave behind. My boyfriend would always make me feel truly guilty. I recall on many occasions him telling me he knew I would never stick by him, how he knew he wasn't good enough for me and how he knew one day I would walk by him on the street, and I would be married with two kids whilst he would still be living the life we were in then. At the time, this used to break my heart and make me feel so much guilt for ever contemplating leaving him. I saw such pain in his face when he shared with me his own visualisation of what the future held. How could he think I would ever leave him? How could he not see that I loved him and would never hurt him like this? Didn't he realise I was going to save us both from this life we were living? Looking back, I see this for what it was, emotional manipulation. He knew that if I ever actually picked my head up and started designing a life for myself, a life I deserved, it would be full of the love that "married with two kids" conjured up for him. He needed to attach guilt and shame to me ever wanting better for myself. This was his way of stopping me wanting what I deserved, the life I have now. It is not lost on me that as I write this chapter I am married with two children. I do not feel any type of guilt for that. I do not feel responsible for his feelings if he ever found out what I have made of my life. The journey to this point was not easy but it was focused, and it was created on purpose, and I deserve every bit of it.

I don't spend much of my time and energy looking back on my past relationships, it often feels like a film I once watched. I know what happened and, as I have done here, I can talk about the facts, but I no longer experience the attached feelings of fear or shame or confusion. There are times, though, that I am thrown back and forced to remember. I recently went out for a day to myself, a truly magical day for a stay-at-home mummy with two under the age of four. I went shopping and then had a fabulous lunch all by myself. I had to sit outside the restaurant, hello 2021, but it was a lovely bright day and sitting outside would have been my preference anyway. I ordered two glasses of rosé wine while I looked at the menu (yes two, I hate waiting for a top up). Once I ordered, I just sat back and took it all in. I started to think about how blessed my life is. I have a supportive husband who pushes me to take days to myself and treat myself while he plays hilarious make-believe games with our two children in our little house that I love. I was almost melting into the chair, so relaxed, without a worry in the world. Then it suddenly came to me, in a really shocking way. The exact street I was sitting on, I saw a vision of myself and two police officers escorting me down that very street. How on earth did I not realise this the moment I got here that I had been here before and the circumstances around it? I saw the shadow of me actually walking down the street and it all came flooding back to me.

That day, over twelve years ago, was the first time my then boyfriend had attacked me in public, outside my work, in front of all my colleagues. My colleagues who had no idea the type of relationship I was in and who were frozen where they stood in the shock of it all. The police had been called that day, my first experience of being a domestic abuse "victim" and everything that comes with that. I was escorted to my car as it was not known where he had gone, and the police did not want to risk a follow-up incident. As I watched this memory play out in front of me, I saw the pain and the embarrassment, but I no longer felt it. I saw a broken woman and I remembered every thought that went through her mind that day, but they were no longer my thoughts, and I was no longer that woman. I took great strength in that moment; I never thought I would be able to remember that incident without feeling it as well.

For me, moving on and creating a life away from abuse doesn't mean forgetting and it doesn't mean pushing the feelings down and not allowing myself to feel them. For me, moving on and creating a new life is replacing those feelings when I do look back with pride and thankfulness for everything I have now. When I watched that twelve-year-old scene play out as a memory, I didn't force myself to block it out or not to feel, but naturally the feelings that bubbled over were overwhelmingly positive and I soon replaced that scene in my mind with me remembering what and who are in my life now.

I still emotionally connect with the women I speak to who have experienced domestic abuse, I still emotionally connect with songs when it feels the lyrics were stolen from my very own thoughts back then, I still connect, I still feel it, but it no longer engulfs me. When I first left, I never ever thought that would be possible, but it absolutely is when you create a life away from abuse. Positive emotions can always overpower negative emotions, light can always shatter darkness.

I founded More to her Life charity in 2020, eleven years after I changed my life. More to her Life delivers gifts and experiences designed to show women that life after domestic abuse can be incredible! I founded this charity to reflect the experience I have had. I have gone from feeling oppressed and in fear to feeling so loved and free and excited about my life. I want to share that feeling with every woman who has experienced an abusive relationship. I understand how difficult it is to dream again and to design a life you are excited to live, and I understand that we sometimes need to be shown a better way before we can truly believe it. I also know visualisation is not for everyone, that is just part of my journey, but the power of connecting an emotion to the life you want to live is going to be life-changing for every single woman leaving an abusive relationship.

The charity gives women a taste of an incredible life to inspire them to keep moving forward towards a future they deserve to have. In 2020 we arranged a trip to a water park for a mother and her teenage son living in a domestic abuse refuge. I wanted them to experience how their lives could be once they rebuilt. This was her feedback:

> "The trip to the water park allowed me and my son a bit of normality and freedom to do what WE wanted to do, without there being an issue and a fight. To see him belly-laugh like he did showed me that we can have a normal life where we can enjoy things and not be scared about what might happen all of the time; thank you so much for arranging it for us!"

That says everything for me. The power of seeing how incredible life can be away from abuse and starting to believe that she can have it and live it daily! I truly hope in her dark times as she moves forward, she reconnects with the emotions from that day and truly allows herself to feel the joy she felt and remember him belly-laughing. Being able to create a charity that mirrors the start of my own journey and helps women to answer their own "what now?!" doubts and fears fills me with such excitement for their futures.

I feel so blessed to have this charity in my life. It was not in my original visualisation, but I took time to see how starting this charity would complement the life I want to live. To be able to stand tall and be a positive part in other women's journeys absolutely brings me feelings of love and such personal fulfilment. Coming out of an abusive relationship, I never thought I would be able to revisit that world without it pulling me back down, which is why I think this type of work never featured in my original visualisation. However, being able to reach back into my past to understand how I rebuilt my life and then mirror that for others actually gives me strength rather than reliving pain.

So, my incredible life away from abuse, I run the charity full time whilst I care for my two confident, happy children and while my caring, supportive husband cares for us all; and yes, he can cook! Do I have the 4x4 and the huge house with the winding driveway from my visions? Not yet.

Do I have all the love and gratitude and freedom I thought that visualisation would bring me?

Abso-bloody-lutely!

Use this space to journal:

Journal questions:

1. Can you describe a simple day in the life you want to live?
2. What promises do you need to make yourself to make sure you are working towards making that a reality?

_____

_____

_____

_____

_____

_____

_____

_____

_____

_____

_____

_____

_____

_____

_____

_____

_____

_____

_____

_____

_____

_____

_____

_____

_____

_____

_____

_____

_____

_____

_____

_____

_____

_____

_____

Do Not Be Defined
By What Happened

Zoe Dronfield

In 2014 I was almost murdered by the man who claimed to love me. You may think this would have destroyed me, however, I have turned this into my superpower and the life I have built after abuse is stronger, richer and I'm more self-assured than ever.

In the initial days after the attack, while still recovering from my injuries plus the shock of what happened in the aftermath (which I will talk about shortly), I sought help from a variety of professionals. All had a part to play in my recovery for different reasons and, without this support, which led to a whole host of understanding and education, I don't know how I would have come through the most horrific ordeal of my life.

It is so important to seek help and not try to go through things alone. There are some fantastic organisations out there that are set up to support you, at any stage of your journey. I think the hardest thing is seeking them out. I had dealt with most things alone my whole life until this point.

I now realise you can gain a lot of strength from others, their stories, their empathy, their validation. You do not have to navigate trauma alone and this was empowering on its own. I'm not saying that everyone who gives you advice will be helpful, however, what I found was by talking to as many people as I could, I found my own answers within their perspective, and this helped enormously.

Since my ordeal, I have grown my network both in business and personally; made new friends, expanded my property portfolio beyond my wildest dreams, excelled in my career, I am on the exec board of Paladin the National Stalking Advocacy Service, I work with the Ministry of Justice in their witness and engagement group and am a regular commentator in the media around domestic abuse and stalking. I have also been a keynote speaker at many conferences and events, so my journey has truly had an impact on my life in more ways than one and in a positive way, which has also helped others and I hope will continue to.

Initially it was hard; I'm not going to lie and tell you it was all easy. However, you must take each day at it comes, especially at the beginning. Self-care is really important, eating well, fitness, going for walks, the gym, or even just giving yourself time out to read a book are key steps to finding yourself again. Going through domestic abuse strips you of your identity and you are thrown into a world that you did not wish to enter.

Education played a huge role in building myself back

up again. I gained confidence and knowledge allowed me to find my strength as it gave me my power back, it highlighted to me that what I went through was not my fault. Self-blame is something all victims may experience, and the education around domestic abuse, stalking, perpetrators of this crime and other victim stories was enlightening and empowering. I read everything I could get my hands on. This helped a great deal.

On the journey to rebuild my life I also sought help from a therapist, specifically to build myself back up. These sessions helped me really focus my mind on where I was going and not on the past. I spoke to many counsellors and support workers before finally deciding on a Cognitive Behavioural Therapist who I decided to work with.

It was important they understood that I wanted to look forward; yes, acknowledge the past and what happened, but lots of counsellors wanted me to unpack everything and go back. The therapist I found was forward focused: Where are you going? What are you doing to improve? Where do you see yourself? Obviously at some time in your journey you may want to address the past but, for me, it was done. Something that happened and that was not going to define me; quite the opposite. As I am a solution-focused person, this approach suited me better than going over and over the attack and why I thought this happened to me. I wanted someone who could help me rebuild. The future was important, not the past.

These sessions involved a lot of work and kept my mind and body busy. We worked on confidence, mindset, fitness, flooding and mood.

Confidence came from the hypnotherapy and reframing what happened to me in the sessions, mindset was focusing on the future and my goals, fitness, well, speaks for itself – but try and find something you enjoy so you stick at it. It's all about a sense of achievement when you keep reaching your goals, however small they need to be in the beginning. Flooding sessions are not for everyone. This is where you are taken back into the scary situation that happened and reframe it with you not as the victim and finding a way to empower yourself. Mood came with all of this work, knowing you are doing so much self-work is mood lifting in itself and fitness definitely helps with this; get the blood moving around your body and air in your lungs. I would also advise anyone getting over trauma to stay away from mood-altering crutches, like alcohol. This is a depressant. Until you are through the worst, it's better to keep a clear head.

I am a strong person by nature. I put this down to losing my mother when I was little. I was six years old, and this gave me resilience from a young age. However, after going through the attack and what happened next with the system, the victim blaming, and my previous ex and father of my daughter (who was four years old at the time) dragging me through family court for custody, I knew I needed help. Everything was stacked against me at this time. I fought on, regardless of the odds.

When I met my perpetrator, I was already successful in my career, had a couple of rental properties and had previously run my own business – although it closed through no fault of my own – so I was already ambitious. However, due to my empathy, my personality and naivety in relationships and due to losing my mother so young, I suppose I was exploited and taken advantage of. The things I could have achieved seemed very far away back then, as my time was taken pandering to the men I was in a relationship with.

I never put myself first.

That has changed. I make a conscious decision to do things based on whether they serve me. It is hard, as my default position is to help others, however, I have to keep myself in check and ensure that whatever I am involved in, using my time for, is ultimately good for me.

The attack and what followed was an epiphany. A realisation that I had given away far too much of myself and needed to move forward, find and rebuild myself.

The recovery began with social media and posting my story online for others to read, understand, empathise with and to inspire. This was extremely empowering and, although I had been shamed by some people who did not understand they were victim blaming at the time, many have since changed their view and realised that by speaking out I am highlighting how domestic abuse affects people's lives and this has helped many, especially those working in the sector.

After speaking at conferences and telling my story, I am often presented with a queue of professionals who want to apologise for the failures of the system and this is exactly why I do what I do, it drives change. After first speaking out,

I was also approached by victims; strangers, people I have known for years, colleagues who all wanted to empathise and share their stories too. It was stark how many people have been affected by domestic abuse and stalking in their lifetime.

I have a Zoe Dronfield public page and also a page called 'I want my mummy', later changed to IWMM. This was created to help other mothers going through family court proceedings with an abusive ex-partner. This was the start of my journey: https://www.facebook.com/iwmm.net/

Talking to victims and survivors of similar ordeals, it compelled me to make changes. I could not stand by and watch anyone else go through what I went through, so I started working with charities and domestic abuse sector professionals to speak out. This work led me to my position at Paladin NSAS.

I was invited by Laura Richards, the founder of Paladin the National Stalking Advocacy Service to join the board. I was honoured and it felt the right thing to do to give back. I support the organisation with media work and strategic direction. The organisation helps hundreds of victims, mainly medium to high risk, and they really specialise in understanding the law and advocating with professionals on behalf of victims. It's invaluable work. There is a real focus on young victims too; currently, we are seeing a lot more online stalking, so this has been a real focus. We are always looking for innovative ways to support victims/survivors. I am so proud of the work we do. Our clients give the staff nothing but praise and we have helped in some very serious situations. It has felt great giving back: https://paladinservice.co.uk/

My campaigning work has led me to go to Downing Street, speak at conferences, give talks in colleges and universities, in parliament. I have been nominated for awards, both by West Midlands Police – oh the irony, that I am now taking WMP to court for their failings. They nominated me for the Bob Jones Community Award for my work in the local area around domestic abuse and I was also nominated for Most Inspiring Person and Local Hero at Pride of Coventry. I have been involved in law change around stalking and domestic abuse and I have delivered sessions with magistrates, regularly speak on the news or in the media. This is both cathartic but also drives change. Being able to tell my story means it is not in my head. I rarely think about what I went through nowadays, only to revisit it to help others or when another issue rears its head. My perpetrator has appealed several times, has been moved to open conditions where I fought to have him put back into closed and is due in front of the parole board soon, so there can often be another trigger; however, I am now mentally and emotionally strong. I actually feel sorry for the people involved in trying to destroy my life because a) it didn't work and b) how miserable must *they* be to exist that way.

Everything I do around domestic abuse and stalking is to help victims/survivors to understand how to reduce their suffering; once you take control back of your mind, your body, your story and your life, there is nothing left for the perpetrator. The good then outweighs the bad. No victim chooses the situation they find themselves in and it's key to keep reminding yourself of that. None of it is your fault.

As a career, in my 'day job', I am an IT consultant working digitalising the NHS and my story has even helped me in my role at work. Management were made aware of my campaigning work and this has been recognised across the business. I have even been nominated for awards this year with CRN Women in Channel Awards 2021. The awards are recognising women in tech and I have been put in for three categories, which I cannot believe, I have total imposter syndrome: Sales Employee of the Year – Reseller/ Solution Provider, Role Model of the Year – Vendor/ Distributor and Woman of the Year. I am blown away, honoured and humbled. My colleagues at Trustmarque (part of Capita) are amazing and a real credit to an amazing company with a strong company ethos of integrity.

Alongside my career and campaigning, I have also grown a property portfolio in Coventry where I live. I already owned a couple of properties before going through my ordeal, as I became an accidental landlord. I closed a business and had to move home with my father which meant I rented my house out purely by accident, I then realised this was another stream of income and gave me security. It was a radio station that made me realise that I could do so much more. I was listening in my car on my way to work one morning when they were talking about stress and the things in life that are most stressful. One of the things they said was the most stressful was buying a house. People can limit you with their beliefs. Watch out for this.

I had to laugh listening, after everything I had been through, I thought 'buying a house is a doddle and I'm going to prove it'. That year I expanded my portfolio buying a further three houses in the same year. A 3-bedroom buy-to-let, a 4-bedroom mini House of Multiple Occupancy (HMO) and a big 7-bed HMO too which required all sorts of regulations to become licensed.

That's the thing with us domestic abuse survivors, we are resilient and have a strength that some people cannot comprehend. Some of us have seen and experienced things that most people only watch in films. Something that could be considered stressful to someone who has never experienced domestic abuse, an abuse victim/survivor would welcome a life of no abuse with maybe an alternative stress. For me its all about mindset.

Learning to put myself first and channel my emotions so they worked for me, as opposed to against me, is my superpower that I have built over time, and this is what I want to share with others. I go into more detail in the book I am currently writing. This documents my journey through life, losing my mother, having a step-family, meeting both abusers. I give tips on what I felt was missing in me, which drove me into these situations and what I have learned from my experiences. I talk about the red flags to look out for when in relationships, how family dynamics play a role in how you evolve emotionally and adapt to things growing up. I really hope it will help others get through the pain barrier and build to be a bigger and better version of themselves, not just surviving but thriving after abuse.

You too can have the life you want, do not be defined by what happened. We are women, we are strong and there is more to MY life than what happened to me in those relationships.

If I can do it, so can you.

Use this space to journal:

Journal questions:

1. How have you ensured self-care throughout your journey? (Made time, reading, conscious thoughts about your well being)
2. What form of self-care has helped you? (ie. exercise, meditation, reading, counselling, speaking out)
3. How would you help your best friend or sister if they had been through a similar ordeal?

_____

_____

_____

_____

_____

_____

_____

_____

_____

_____

_____

_____

_____

The Long Way Home

Liberty Santiago

Hello love! If you are reading this, you have probably been through some traumatic experiences in your life. I am inviting you to do a little exercise with me to kick off this chapter. Look around you now. Are you in a safe space? Safe enough to be reading this message? I think you can agree it is a gift from the universe. Granted, not everything in your circumstances will feel like a gift, even if it has been years since your trauma. In fact, you could right now have a tremendous amount of mental anguish, feelings of loss and, perhaps, even physical pain. I want you to know I see you, hear you and I choose to show up with love and compassion for you and your family. It is safe to be seen with pain and to ask for help. You are not broken, and you don't need fixing. You are not too much and you're worthy of others supporting you, so you fully become who you were actually meant to be in this life. This book is a sign, a message, and confirmation of your worthiness. You will heal and your life will get better. You have the power to choose.

Breathwork has many benefits, and you can do it

anywhere, even if you don't have lots of time. Take a deep breath through your mouth, filling your lungs and your belly. Hold your breath in at the top for three seconds and let it go! Repeat this three times. With each breath settle into the state of gratitude, letting go of thoughts and feelings that distract you. Focus now on three things that make you feel safe, seen, and worthy. Write down three things you can be grateful for. You will be glad you did!

1.

2.

3.

Okay, now that I have shared with you one powerful tool I use every day, I am encouraging you to try it out for size and see if the tool of breathwork and gratitude is a good fit for you. If they are, I encourage you to use them in your daily life. Having a daily routine that makes me feel good has helped me find my happiness.

Check in with yourself about how you are feeling before and after the exercise. Are you a bit more relaxed and focused? Take note of where you feel tension in your body. All your feelings are clues. As simple as it sounds, find yourself a 'feelings' word list, one that you like, and tape it to the inside of a notebook or in a binder. Learn to identify your feelings beyond the main categories like anger, sadness, fear, love, joy and surprise. This helps you with creating self-awareness.

We have six higher mental faculties and one of them is the will in the mind. Trauma and feelings are also connected to physical tension or even pain that manifests in your body. You can discover a pattern of feelings and where you hold pain in your body. Once you become aware, you can invite intentional healing in a way that feels good to you. By focusing on the way you want to experience your life and how you want to feel, you can start to change the way you experience life. Practicing a little each day, focusing on what is going well in your reality is buildable and creates momentum. Spend time each day visualizing your new life and who you become when you choose differently and think differently. Exercise your higher mental faculties to reach outside of the familiar reel that plays on the screen in your mind.

You have the power to choose a new story by creating the new picture with your imagination, but this is not fantasy, this is your real life that is all preceded by thoughts. You might think about how your new story won't be supported by this person or that person. Instead of letting that person's opinion of you make you feel small, accept that not everyone can see the vision for your new life, and that is okay. Not everyone gets to be a character in your new picture. That is the exciting part of our human design: our ability to create. Even if you don't have a plan and cannot explain how, invite the idea that everything you need will show up at the time it is meant to —while you do your healing, your happiness is processing. This idea is a broad yet valuable outline for self-help, one I did not learn in recovery or small group sessions.

I didn't always care how the mind worked. Not until I

realized the way I was experiencing my life was a reflection of how my mind operated: in the negative. It took me an extremely long time to admit I had been thinking about my life all wrong. I was operating on old programming and poor beliefs about my self-worth. The things I was taught growing up and the circumstances as I perceived them all contributed to this narrative that was not aligned to the life I desired to live. One of the challenges I had a tough time with was accepting that justice would not be given to my abuser quickly or as I had expected. I learned the only real control I had was the control over my own thinking. I had to become the change I wanted to see, not just in the world but in my own world. These are just a few of the lessons I learned.

I want to share with you my story of how I transformed my life after abusive relationship cycles. Through my lens looking back, I get to share with you, my friend, some golden strands of truth. My intention is to provide a view into my story, which you may relate to, along with some tips to help you find your happiness.

If you are anything like me, you had so many thoughts going on in your mind each time you were ready to end the abuse. Thinking of solutions, let alone reading about them, was not on my list of instinctual things to do as I began my journey to reclaim my worth. I want to commend you for investing in yourself and reading this book. Hopefully, I can teach you a few things I wish I would have known looking back. Perhaps someone will make similar suggestions to you, or perhaps you begin to note a similar theme throughout these chapters among the different authors. If it feels redundant, perhaps it is so, but it is impactful.

Did you know constant spaced repetition or emotional impact are the two ways that beliefs are changed? Hearing what works over and over again will help to form a new way of thinking. Our conscious mind only absorbs a fraction of what we hear, taste, feel, touch and see, and when we are filled with fear, doubt and worry, we absorb even less. Our minds look for – and in some instances even create – an illusion based on what our mind believes, our perception. Don't worry about remembering everything you read, there is no test at the end. Take the opportunity to implement the ideas into your life if and when what you read resonates. Perhaps what you read today won't make a change because our minds have to be ready for the change. You will even come back to this chapter one day in your mind and recall a fresh perspective, tool, or the voice of a friend you can relate to as you grow through the challenges that lie ahead.

There have been many challenges on my path to becoming the woman I am today. I know that I have taken lessons, awareness and personal growth from each and every painful, thrilling and dangerous event. I have seen people of all walks of life experience challenges. There is a meaningful connection and a healing power that is exchanged when you are able to relate with another who has similar challenges, like abuse, which we have experienced as women and perhaps as mothers as I did. I invite you to listen for the similarities in our stories as you can more easily imagine yourself healed and happy. Know that if I can heal and thrive, so can you.

You can use the stories in these chapters as a source of guidance from someone who has been there where you are, starting over, afraid and stripped of the comforts of knowing how life used to be and the unknown of how life is going to be, looking ahead. I want you to know that nothing is too hard to walk through on the way to meeting the next best version of yourself. Becoming the best version of you is the single best investment you can make for your life and it is benefiting your family directly each day that you wake up and choose yourself. You are worth every step and challenge that you get to walk through. I invite you to explore the idea that you are embarking on a beautiful journey of choices that includes the ability to love yourself today, right where you are at. Despite the imperfections of circumstance, you get to find gratitude, joy and self-love along the way rather than focusing on the pain. Your feelings are a gift. Feel your feelings, identify them and make meaning from what they are telling you based on where you want to be five years from now.

I want to start with my childhood. I think I was born stubborn, creative and willful, I knew what I wanted and wasn't afraid to ask. I was born to my parents, who had been divorced for three months, and to a brother who was six years my elder. As a single family, my mom, myself and older brother lived with my paternal grandmother, a widow by the age of 49. I was in the second grade when my mother got a job in law enforcement ninety miles away.

Shortly after we relocated, my brother moved back in with our grandma because he felt isolated and had a hard time adjusting to a new friendship group in junior high. My great grandparents sponsored my education in a private school from the time we moved to high school. My mom stayed single until about the time I was in middle school when she met and married my stepdad. I recall my mother working all the time. I spent time enjoying art and sports, including dance and performing arts. I did spend lots of time with myself as the only child in our home, and I valued my space to be creative. I would find neighborhood kids to play with and had some school friends that lived close by.

I started having a regular relationship with my father when I was in the sixth grade. I would spend every other weekend and summers traveling ninety minutes each way to fulfil the custody time with my father. For much of that time I stayed with my grandma and my father would drop by for a visit. Occasionally, my father planned fishing trips or professional soccer games for us to attend. I have mostly good memories from my childhood. I did not learn until I was about twenty-six years old that my father had a problem with alcohol, from which he has now recovered.

In my case, the pattern of unhealthy abusive relationships began as a young teen when I began choosing romantic relationships of my own. I grew up hearing that children who are abused are attracted to abusive relationships as an adult, which makes sense to me. However, I was unable to relate to this statistic knowing I had not been involved in mentally, emotionally, or physically abusive relationships as a child.

I think you can agree that healthy relationships are not taught in school. Relationships are demonstrated in real life. How we observe and interact with relationships as a child is crucial to our understanding of what healthy and unhealthy relationships look like. From the time I was a teen, I had been conducting a real-life experiment, collecting data of what unhealthy relationships looked and felt like. Meanwhile, I was discovering the depths of the consequences these abusive relationships would have on myself and my children born into them. My life with abusive male relationships lasted a little over twenty years. I had experienced several dozen relationships that included drug and alcohol abuse, mental, physical and emotional abuse. As a consenting person, sexual boundaries were crossed in most of these relationships. It was not one relationship that was unhealthy in my case, it was all of them. I spent a lot of time confused, asking myself, "What is wrong with me? Why is my life full of disappointment and abuse?" The context of never being physically or sexually abused as a child would leave me in the dark about why I chose these abusive relationships. It wasn't until I did some deep mental and emotional freedom healing a few years back that I finally realised why.

From my time in private school, I learned a lot about what the Bible says about love and that we are treasured as his children. In times of darkness, I drew on thoughts from my Bible study, particularly what God says about me. I used this learning and eventually developed faith in action as I turned away from unhealthy relationships. Each step of transformation had a level of discomfort, yet it was liberating and confirming to realise that there is a life full of beauty, pleasure and real love like the Bible said. I discover my own power, strength and ability to discern and make decisions based on my intuition.

My longest relationship to date was with an abuser who had his claws in me by mental and emotional abuse. In this relationship, I would find myself the victim of identity and personality suppression. I would take on his debt, fall into the allure of all his big ideas while permitting his career to be the compass for our life. I became the leap pad for his successes and our relationship would take on the mask of romance and power. I was co-dependent on him for fulfillment, entertainment, pleasure, permission and I found my identity in the relationship with him. As my abuser became stronger in his identity while climbing the corporate ladder as a highly paid executive, his need for me diminished. The relationship left me exhausted, defeated and lost. I rarely recall praying during this relationship. I felt devoured and lost. We went to church only once together. I begged him to go to a non-denominational church with me. He went to show me how it would not practically fit into our lifestyle. During the service, there was a women's ministry event that piqued my interest. I mentioned how I might like to attend, and he laughed about how unrealistic that was considering how busy we were with his family and career events.

He began traveling for weeks at a time, rarely available to talk on the phone, and dismissive of the needs of the family. In times of need, he would remind me of the importance of his vision and what needed to be sacrificed for success at that scale. I felt dismissed, unseen and unheard, over and over again. I became the interest of another influential man in my life. I fell into the emotional escape of the affair that was being offered. One day, my abuser found messages about the proposed affair, and it was then that I became the center of the blame. I believed it. All of it. The guilt and shame had my head hung lower than the pain of being unseen and unheard. I was "the problem". I was given an ultimatum to get treatment from a psychologist and psychiatrist or end the relationship. Like any co-dependent partner who feels guilt, I did what I was told. I had multiple weekly visits, intensive therapy, multiple mental wellness providers, couples therapy and child therapy.

Two and a half years later, more sexual boundaries had been crossed with and without my abuser, all of which were my fault according to him. I was on many different prescriptions to manage "my problem". Deprived of all personal interest and flogged with guilt, I hit my rock bottom. All my energy was drained, poured into this toxic relationship where I accepted all blame. I was spiritually blocked and unable to focus on anything. My mental anguish and physical pain were caused by the side effects of the prescribed medications. According to my abuser and the providers, these medications were keeping me safe. I could only think that I was "the problem".

I remember laying on my couch hidden away in the back of the house away from my abuser and away from our family. I was lying there feeling completely broken and alone, not able to cry or process feelings anymore, just existing and collecting enough energy to go to work the next day... As I lay there so totally blank and confused, I vividly remember my inner voice telling me to get off all those pills so I could think again, feel connection again, and heal the trauma from years of abuse the way our human bodies are designed to! I was scared because my abuser would constantly repeat that I should continue going to the doctors and taking the prescribed medications. I understood that he was threatening that if I stood up for myself and got off the pills, I would potentially be sacrificing my relationship, my family, my support, everything I had known for the past nine and half years.

Changing your life is scary. It requires us to dig deep and do something that we have not done before and think in a new way. Then, if you were to tell me what challenges I would go through to become the woman I am today, I would have been full of fear and overwhelm. Perhaps you feel that way now or have felt that yourself at some times throughout your journey. However, the more important message is that today, looking back to connect the dots, I can safely say each step was worth it. I am worth the challenges and lessons that were a part of my journey just like you are worth walking through your challenges and lessons. I discovered that we are never alone and the voice inside of our higher self can be trusted.

That day on the couch, I called a recovery hotline from a commercial that played on the television. That day I took responsibility for my life. I was scared then, too. I made the arrangements, took a leave of absence from work, and focused the next thirty days on getting off the prescriptions that were, in my opinion, a huge part of the problem. One of the challenges I faced was receiving the support I felt I deserved. My abuser told me that I didn't need to go and recover. He told me that I just needed to take the medication and that part of my problem was thinking that I could ever be off them. Because I wore a mask of wealth, romance and unity, my parents and a few close friends were confused and did not relate or support me, not knowing the history and suppression. I was afraid that I was overthinking my circumstances or that my abuser was right, but my intuition kept telling me otherwise.

I went through with my recovery plan. I went away to recovery and that is where I briefly met myself again and discovered my spiritual connection. Throughout my journey, I truly learned what faith meant. I flew across the country to detox from the medications and start learning about sobriety. Although my family and abuser did not understand, I went forward for me. I made an agreement with my abuser to return a better version of me and he agreed to my absence and the restoration of our relationship when I came back. I did not make it easy on myself as I fought the process and attempted to negotiate with myself and counselors that I made a mistake. I did turn away from the plan about five days into it. I was feeling unsupported and disconnected from the safety of home and family. I felt something was terribly wrong in the voice of my abuser during a call while I was away. I decided to come home early. My mom picked me up from the airport. I went home to collect clothes appropriate for our fall weather and see the family. I called my abuser to let him know I made it back home and I would be transitioning to a local recovery house to be closer to the family. He informed me that I would find that the locks on the door to our home had been changed and that I was cut off from the family. I was literally shut out, labeled and filled with fear! In fact, a huge challenge was that I lived that way for years during and after leaving this abusive relationship. I was ashamed! I was so defensive, bitter, afraid of discovering myself, and confused as to why life seemed so unjust... I went for years feeling this way! I held on to so much of that guilt and shame for the way things ended and how others viewed me. This was really the beginning of the hardest road I've ever had to walk. The hard part wasn't sobriety, it was losing my family while finding myself weighed down with fear from my abuser and the other abusive relationships I experienced along the way.

I had only a few weeks left before I had to return to work from my leave of absence. I found a sober living home and admitted myself. I learned I had been locked out and cut off with no choice in the matter of returning home to be with my family pending a long legal battle. I felt out of control and uncared for. I remember my abuser coming to drop off the belongings he would allow me to have at the sober living house. He dismissed any care for me or my feelings and was not there to visit. I went inside and felt so totally helpless. I thought no one cared for me. One of the daytime counselors shared with me Peter 5:7 "Cast all your anxiety on him because he cares for you." Even though it was hard to accept, I was surrendering my relationship and feelings of unworthiness to God with faith that he would use this for my good. I knew that my sobriety and this separation was a big undertaking and at the time I had no idea how it would all happen. I trusted in the plan God had for me. I trusted God was there for me and my family even though the direction I was taking was the unpopular choice. It was hard for people in my life to support me because I had kept so much private. It was hard for anyone to understand what my pain was really like. I made it hard for myself because I only trusted God with the long game and with little pieces of me at a time. A significant challenge I faced was that I was willing to go deep with healing myself, but I had the tendency to shy away from seeing it through due to shame, self-preservation and feelings of injustice.

I would continue to make unhealthy relationship choices. I transitioned from the recovery home to start back at work again. Fearful of living with my mother at the age of thirty, I decided to start a romantic relationship with one of the men from the sober living home. After knowing him for only a few weeks we were living together. That relationship was short-lived and ended with life-threatening events. When that one ended, another one like it formed. This was the cycle for me, almost an unconscious compulsion: escaping one abuser to find myself being attracted to another abuser in different forms. The abusive relationships were a cycle for me, unknowingly I found comfort in the chaos. I would start a relationship with a man who had a toxic background and find that I was convincing myself that they had changed or would continue to change for the better. In little to no time, I would be in a sexual relationship with them and living with these toxic men. They were driven by ego, drugs and alcohol. Once they crossed my boundaries and were abusive, I would attempt to fix it and they would attempt to control the outcome for fear that I would leave. They used lies, verbal abuse, assault, theft, threats against my life and guilting me. They blamed me, saying that I was the one who made them do it. Once I identified these relationships as toxic, abusive, or dangerous, my wounded human ego would not allow me to walk away without a tripwire life-threatening event occurring. Each time I left more wounded, guarded and ashamed.

The turning point for me was mentorship. Since separating from the first abuser in my story I had been actively involved in Alcoholics Anonymous and Celebrate Recovery for my sobriety. These programs of sobriety are supportive time-tested programs for living. I followed what the programs said to do. I got involved, showed up consistently, built relationships, took leadership roles, and worked the twelve-step program with a sponsor. I did the twelve steps as honestly as I could. Despite being in unhealthy relationships, I maintained a program of sobriety and found healthy support, accountability partners, and events to help myself.

I had a few different mentors and some of the truths that were reflected back to me during our one-to-one time were shocking and hard to accept. My first mentor in recovery told me a truth that I don't think I was honestly ready to hear at the time and it would take three more years to learn what she meant by it. She told me, "Based on what you share with me, you seem to be living a double life." She explained what she heard was that inside I desired peace, calm and family restoration, but on the outside, I lived loosely and the very opposite of the goals I said I wanted. She warned that only one could win out, either the outside circumstance or the inside desire. I didn't speak to her again. There again was my tendency to turn away from my healing due to shame. I could not bear to hear the truth because I was unwilling to implement the changes I needed to break the cycle of abusive relationships. I had not yet started my twelve-step program and I would delay my growth by sitting with my wounded human ego, afraid to uncover more dispelling truths about me. Going to group meetings regularly helped me. I stayed plugged in and I listened for similarities.

I had ongoing fear and was constantly subjected to negative labels by the first abuser mentioned in my story. I felt confused and I wanted to make meaning of it, but when I found myself obsessing over it, I held on to the verse that I rediscovered in a recovery meeting: "For I know the plans I have for you," declares the Lord, "Plans to prosper you and not to harm you, plans to give you hope and a future." (Jeremiah 29:11) I wanted healing and restoration. I allowed myself to find friends and give back inside the program. I allowed myself to invite a second mentor into my life. I was attracted to her presence of peace, her calmness of mind, and her story of restoration after four marriages. She would meet with me one on one in a coffee shop and she would listen to me without judgment. She would reflect back to me, and I felt seen and heard. She helped me a lot with accepting the way things are for me as a mother. After being separated from my abuser, my relationship with our children was limited. She taught me to be grateful for the relationship I did have with my children and trust that though it didn't look like the "normal" family, nothing has the power to separate our love, not the other parent, nor time or distance – much like the unconditional love of God. She also helped me to pull back the veil on yet another toxic relationship I was in at the time. I was in a relationship with my second live-in boyfriend who I met in recovery. I had a hard time seeing the abuse in this relationship. I desperately wanted it to be different this time. She supported me and my decision to end it.

I had done the twelve steps and I was sober. I had stability and consistency. Unfortunately, my boyfriend had not gone through the steps of his recovery, had no mentor, and was hiding who he was from me. I saved my life by ending the last two relationships as both had threatened and planned on taking my life. I was a good mother in those moments by choosing to start over again on my quest to discover the best version of me. However, this time was different. This time I was emotionally supported by my mentor and accountability partners from recovery.

I started a small life group from the women in the program who were my accountability partners, who felt like sisters to me. We met at my house on Sunday mornings to study ourselves through God's eyes. We would share some breakfast and share our hearts using the worksheet answers. I started to have consistent healthy friendships with other women for the first time in my life. We found relatability in that we were also all single with children at the time. I was counted on, I was treasured and I was receiving love in a healthy way.

I committed to and went through the twelve-step program for the second time. This time more thoroughly than the last. I had also committed to my version of being single. For me, that was dating and having relationships with men without the intention of sex. I found that I had made a sport of it, which was eventually exhausting, and I knew that was not what God wanted for me. Although exciting and thrilling at times, I felt drained and unappreciated through my serial dating. I also found myself overly interested in a man who was not emotionally available, and I ended up getting hurt again. My mentor encouraged me to study the book *Boundaries in dating*. It was through these experiences and studying that book that I developed the intention of dating to find the one! I created a list of non-negotiables that a mate would have to have in order to be considered as the one. I redirected my efforts from allowing just anyone to walk into my life to the intention of finding the one and only person I wanted to be with.

I stopped dating and stopped looking. I abstained from having sex for the longest recorded time of my life. I cried myself to sleep sometimes and felt lonely and afraid. I prayed to God with surrender and faith, believing that he has not forgotten me, and I knew he was preparing the right man for me. Clinging onto the truth in Jeremiah 29:11, I knew there must be more to my life than this. My mentor explained that my feelings were a normal part of the healing process and that, in her experience, she found loneliness to be a choice. She explained to me that she actually enjoyed her alone time. When she shared that, my mind recalled my alone time as a child where I was free to be creative. She encouraged me to be expressive with art and listen to positive music, go on shopping dates with myself, and even write things in my journal. I was born stubborn, and I gracefully accepted this part of my design, so I did not always adhere to the suggestions, but I found myself feeling more and more confident. Then clarity came. I was no longer distracted by any relationship at the time, I finally had space for myself. I started doing things for myself. I began exercise classes three times a week and made my self-care more of a priority. Nothing too extravagant but a bubble bath, face mask, pedicure, or coffee and chat with a friend here and there greatly helped.

Investing the time in myself with the program of recovery was not complicated. The hardest part was making the commitment to implementing the changes in my life and walking with faith: taking the action even when my mind told me I didn't want to. This is why mentorship has been so beneficial in making life changes, which for me have been positive and permanent. No one can take away your personal power once you are healed. As I grow as a woman of good character, my challenges are far less life-threatening or draining.

After a short time of surrender, I attracted a relationship with a man who is still my partner today. He exceeds my list of non-negotiables and shows me unconditional love and support. It was through him that I discovered even more personal growth and healing. As progressive thinkers, he and I share a fascination with becoming the best version of ourselves. He introduced me to the works of some of the greatest thought leaders of our time who are featured in the hit movie *The Secret.* Together we read and study ourselves. Some of the teachings to discover are from Napoleon Hill, Earl Nightingale and Raymond Holliwell.

My story of thriving after abuse stems from escaping it. It was only after I consciously ended the abusive relationship cycle that I could discover true healing. Since I decided to invest in myself by completing the twelve-step program and meeting with my mentor regularly, my life has never been the same. I have advanced to going through with alternative healing modalities such as mindset training, mental and emotional freedom technique, hypnosis, EFT Tapping, meditation, breathwork, healing frequencies, Reiki and adopting a self-care routine.

Every time I made a decision to invest in my highest good and acted on it, God and the universe responded to meet my needs. Even in the eleventh hour when doubt creeps in, I allow myself to find assurance that everything I need to heal and thrive in life will be made available for me. I have found faith to be a nice shady tree to rest under on a hot day. It is a familiar place to land. The truth is that we are worth so much more than chaos, control and confusion. The distraction of toxic people in our life or toxic substances is by design to keep us small and suffering. It is our job to draw on our higher mental faculties, including intuition and the will to see change through. The journey begins with the ability to see our part. Through acceptance of what tendencies and personality traits we have, we can begin the healing journey on our pathway to peace.

In the programs and life group, I found myself writing things down. I was taking part in the study of myself. I learned how I wanted relationships to be a part of my life and who I wanted to become inside these relationships that are important to me. I reframed my feelings of loss when thinking about my children, making sure they have the tools to heal themselves and break the cycle in their life. The gift I get to give my children is them seeing their mother rise from my version of rock bottom and starting over time after time to create a life worthy of living. I may not have all the time I wanted with my children, but nothing can separate them from the gift of learning how to show up for yourself in the face of fear.

Today, it is a very, very different story. I remember praying for what my life looks like today. The healthy, thriving woman I am makes decisions that are based on a greatly improved self-image.

Right now, I am curled up on my couch in a neighborhood best known in our city for being peaceful. I am grateful, journaling and calling out to the kids to settle down their wild laughter in their room full of games. My daughter has been in my care full time for the last five years. These days, I have had more time with my youngest child than any other year since being separated as his primary caregiver. My days are committed to personal, professional growth and maintaining mental wellness. I am now thriving and enjoying the life that I designed through the commitment I made to myself. I am now a full-time entrepreneur and make a living from programs of deep life changing impact for my clients. Success is rooted in the fulfillment of my new life. I always begin my achievements with imagining my new story, then I begin to reverse engineer, all the while holding on to faith that one day my dreams will become a reality as I keep showing up for myself. Each accomplished version of myself births another version of me more aware, more impactful and trusting that there is always more to my life.

Use this space to journal:

Journal questions:

1. Imagine the woman you want to become in 5 years, what advice does she give you today?
2. In what areas of your life does improvement feel easy?
3. In what areas of your life do you already feel supported?
4. Are you ready to allow yourself to feel longer periods of happiness today?
5. Can I love myself and accept myself exactly as I am today?

Letting LOVE into My Life

Amanda Acker

My heart is racing, and my palms are sweating as if I have just finished running for miles. I feel like everything around me is closing in and I do not know how I will ever cross the finish line. My mind is telling me that I cannot do this, and I must stay where I am, because if I do not, I will lose everything. I will never be able to make it on my own.

It is freezing cold outside, the kind of day that you just want to crawl under a million blankets and sip on hot coffee. After running to my daughter's daycare to pick her up, I flew to my house. Here I am rushing, throwing whatever I can into garbage bags and leaving most of my possessions behind. I close the door behind me and run to my car heaving these incredibly heavy bags into the trunk and backseat along with my daughter Luckily my son was not with us and was safe at school. Speeding off, tears are crashing into my lap, and I cannot catch my breath. As my house gets smaller in the rear view, I start to feel calmer. The tears are getting less heavy, and I feel a glimmer of hope.

Arriving at the shelter, I can feel all the women's eyes on me, and I feel like a huge fraud. They have been through way worse than me, I tell myself. Who am I to be here? My mind is telling me to just go back, it will be easier to stay. But then I am welcomed with open arms and handed the essentials that I will need to survive. In that moment, I knew I was where I needed to be.

Going down to the room I was assigned, I felt this overwhelming sense of calm. I no longer had to worry about getting yelled at or reminded of how horrible I was. I no longer needed to cry myself to sleep in fear of what would happen the next day. This was the start of my new life, and I was never going back.

I made a promise to myself back then, I was never going to allow another man into my life on a deep level. I was going to keep whoever it was at arm's length and not allow him to meet my children. I was going to create a bubble for us to stay in and no one was allowed in. We were on our own and I was determined to keep it that way.

Soon after arriving at the shelter, I moved to my own apartment. I felt like I had finally made it into true adulthood. It was just me taking care of everything, paying the bills, making sure my kids were fed and safe, and keeping our new home spotless. What I thought was a dream come true quickly turned into a nightmare. I was not sleeping, and I felt more alone than I had in my entire life. This feeling of loneliness led me to a dark place.

I started to think about love. I started to analyze all my past relationships and quickly realized that no one ever genuinely loved me. Each relationship started and ended the same. They started with me falling in love so quickly that my friends would tell me I was crazy. I would make my life all about the person I was with and was always trying to fix them. They would tell me they loved me too and I believed them all. I made countless sacrifices for the men that I loved, including being the only one working and paying for everything, down to their underwear. I thought that was what love was. I thought I had to be everything in the relationship and get nothing in return. Over time it would escalate to where I was being tormented or beaten on a regular basis. I was called all the names in the book, and I cried more than I laughed for most of my adult life.

All these relationships ended with me losing everything and having to start over again. I would have to pack my bags and leave my home in fear. I never had money and would end up with another man who would do the same. It was a never-ending cycle of despair.

After thinking about this, I concluded that I simply did not deserve love. I was never going to have a normal relationship. I would never have a man who loved me for me or have a true partnership. I was devastated to say the least.

There was this day that I could not stop the tears and I just wanted to end it all. I was convinced that, no matter what I did, I would always be crying more than laughing. I knew I could not end my life because I had my children to think of. No matter what pain I was feeling, they needed me, and I had to figure out how to pull myself together.

I did the only thing I knew to do and that was to call my friends and tell them how I was feeling. Within a blink of an eye, they were at my apartment with hugs and pizza. It was the first thing to put a smile on my face in quite some time.

I talked to them for hours about how I was never going to be able to find anyone to love me. The tears came back with a vengeance as I described to them how horrible I was feeling. They insisted that none of what I was saying was true and reminded me of how brave I was for leaving. In this moment, my mind would not allow me to believe them, but somehow it helped me to stop crying.

We continued talking and then the subject of a mutual friend came up. Well, I guess I cannot say mutual friend. He was close with them, and I had known him for years, but we did not exactly get along. But I always had this gut feeling that we would end up together. As we talked about him, I was telling my friends how much I wished I had been nicer to him and how I doubted he would even want to talk to me. As soon as the words came out of my mouth, one friend had him on video chat. My nerves instantly started to knot, and I had no idea what I would even say to him if the camera was pointed in my direction. As soon as I had that thought, *bam*! The camera was on me. My makeup was smeared all over my face and my eyes were still wet from all the tears. I was embarrassed to say the least. As soon as his eyes met mine, I felt electricity, like we were already connected. His blue eyes pierced my soul and I wanted him next to me. The exchange was awkward, and

I do not think either of us truly knew what to say, so it was a short, small talk conversation. He told me his phone was dying but gave me his number.

After we hung up, I told my friends how nervous I was and was not sure if I should contact him or not. They encouraged me to reach out to him, but I was still not sure if I should. Eventually, my friends left, and it was time for me to go to bed. I remember lying there staring at his number in my phone. I then made the brave decision to text him, "I think you're cute." I instantly felt the butterflies in my stomach and was unsure if I made the right decision. A short time went past and then my phone went off and there he was texting me back. Oh, my goodness, I felt like a teenager again! We talked for a little while and I slept that night.

From that day forward, we talked all day every single day. I was still unsure of all of this, and my mind kept reminding me that I did not deserve love and that he would end up like all the other men who have hurt me in the past. It was too good to be true, like someone calling me and telling me I won a million dollars, but then finding out it was a scam.

A week or so later, my friends were having a fire and invited us both. The excitement and nervousness of seeing him in person was overwhelming. I went to work the day of the fire and brought my change of clothes, because who wants to wear flats at a fire with the man that gives you mad butterflies? Driving to their apartment I almost convinced myself to turn around and just go home. Luckily, I did not, and that night was the start of our love story.

Upon arriving at the fire, I bolted into their apartment and changed into my favorite jeans and T-shirt. I snapped some photos with my son and their daughter and acted as if I was not excited for him to arrive, even though I could barely stand the butterflies in my stomach. When he finally arrived, I remember how awkward we were around each other. Even though we had been talking for days, in person the nervous energy between the two of us was overwhelming. As the night went on, I asked him if he wanted to get out of there and go to a bar by my apartment. He agreed and then we drove away in separate cars, my son stayed with his Dad. He followed me to my place because I wanted to walk to the bar with him, since it was only a few blocks away.

When we got there, I invited him in because I wanted to show him my place. We started talking and I was telling him all about my current situation and how I was feeling about love. We never went to the bar and spent all night talking. I had not laughed and smiled so much in an awfully long time. He made me feel human and, even though I was telling him some dark stuff, he did not judge me and reassured me that everything was going to be okay. This man who I had not treated well in the past was sitting in my apartment telling me I was worth having love in my life. I could not believe it, how could someone so good even want to be in the same room as me, let alone behind a locked door? I was dumbfounded, but at the same time really did not want him to leave. I knew in that moment that I could not lose him.

We did not kiss or even cuddle that night, we simply talked

as friends. I did not want to scare him off, so I did not tell him how much I liked him or how I did not want him to leave. As soon as he walked out the door to go home, I wanted him to come back. It was like we were connected by an invisible piece of string. Luckily, he felt the same and we hung out again very soon after that night. This time was a bit different.

It was a Friday night and since I was working at an accounting firm and it was tax season, I had to go to work on Saturday. We did not plan on staying up late, but when 5am rolled in, I needed to get some sleep. We were on my couch, so I asked him if it was okay if I lay down with him. As I lay my head on his chest and could hear his heartbeat, I felt so safe and warm. I fell asleep and my alarm went off shortly after. I nudged him awake and told him I had to get ready for work. Both of us were disappointed and honestly just wanted to get more sleep. As I walked him to the door we hugged, but this hug was different and, when we locked eyes, something magical happened and we kissed. This kiss was one that made my foot pop up as if it had a mind of its own. The sparks were flying, and I did not want it to end. My heartbeat to a different tune that day and, shortly after, we officially became boyfriend and girlfriend.

Unfortunately, we did not ride off into the sunset like you see in the movies. Even though I was on cloud nine, so to speak, I still had my baggage, and it quickly came to the surface. My self-doubt and lack of trust had an impact on our relationship to the point of almost breaking it. My past was trying extremely hard to destroy my present.

My phone was buzzing and when I looked to see what

was so urgent, I saw the words flash on my screen. My past was back to haunt me, and it was relentless. Message after message telling me how horrible I was and that my amazing new boyfriend was worthless and was going to hurt me. The incessant reminder that I was a bad person and should not be with the person who made my heart light up. I was being pulled in too many directions and my mind was being clouded with pain and doubt. The tear-filled days were back, and I started to fall back into depression. I felt so much guilt and could not believe I allowed this wonderful man into my life when I still had so much to work through. He did not deserve to live this life with me.

He did not leave, but instead tried desperately to get me to see that what my past was telling me was not true and that his love for me was never going to end. He would tell me that I could trust him and to listen to what he was saying. My mind would not allow me to believe his words and I fought with him instead of embracing his love. In hindsight, I simply did not think I deserved such a pure love, so I was subconsciously pushing him away, thinking I was protecting him.

None of this made him leave and I could not understand why he wanted to stay. This made me start to think that he was exactly like all the other men I loved and was going to hurt me anyway. I was not listening to him and kept listening to my past and it was causing a lot of stress on our relationship. I was no longer on cloud nine, I was crashing like an airplane in a bad storm, and I did not think I was going to survive.

To my surprise, he was still there; as angry as he was, as much as I tried to push him away, he persisted. He held me as I fell to the ground in tears over what my past was telling me. He cleaned my apartment when I could not get myself out of bed. He carried me through one of the most difficult moments of my life.

Amidst all of this, when I was at my lowest, he married me. I could not understand still how he could love me, and I was not even sure if I fully trusted him to not hurt me. But my heart knew it was the right thing to do and that I could not let him walk out of my life. We did not have a wedding, but it was still one of the happiest days of my life. I did not think about the past that day and only saw our future together after the storm settled.

You see, his love did not lessen when I was sad or mad. His love was constant and grew more each day. My husband was not like the other men I had loved. His eyes looked into my soul and saw me as someone who deserved love. He listened to my painful stories and never once questioned me. He allowed me to be me freely with no judgement. I was not used to this kind of love, it was overwhelming, but in a good way.

At this point I was still uneasy and could not allow myself to fully let his love in. When I told him how I was feeling, he did not yell or walk away from me like I was used to. Instead, he started to ask me questions to figure out why I could not fully trust him yet. He held me in his arms and allowed me to openly talk about my feelings and the reasons why I felt the way I did. He gave me advice on how to trust and reminded me again and again that he was not going to leave me. I could not believe that for once in my life I mentioned my feelings and did not have to end up defending myself or arguing. It was the breath of fresh air I needed.

Soon after, I lost my job at the accounting firm, and I had no idea what to do. I was so used to being the only one paying bills and taking care of everything. I was afraid to tell him because I was not sure if it would end up in an argument with me having to figure it all out on my own. I called him to let him know because, even though I was afraid, I knew I could not keep it from him. He was not mad and did not yell at me. He told me it was going to be okay, and we would talk about it when he got home. I started to clean the apartment because I am one of those odd people who finds cleaning relaxing. My husband came home and, with no words, just held me and let me cry. We spent the next few days figuring out how we could replace the income and, as a team, made it work.

Again, his love for me did not change and he never once made me feel bad about what had happened. This made my mind change gears. I started to really look at our marriage and how, even when things were bad, his love remained. Mind you, this all happened within the first year of our marriage. Crazy to think that he loved me that much so early on, that he did not leave. I needed to change how I looked at love and, more importantly, trust.

After being in toxic relationships for so many years, it was hard for me to accept the fact that someone could love me for me. It seemed so unrealistic. All these questions would pop up in my mind, like, "When will he start hurting me?" "If I open my heart and fully allow myself to trust him, will that be when he starts treating me differently?" Every time these questions came up, I would freeze in fear. I did not want to lose this love that was shining over me, but my fear was still holding me back.

Our marriage started to feel like a storm, and I did not know when the rainbow was going to appear. My fears and self-doubt led me to even more toxic relationships that could have torn us apart. I was influenced by these new people – my "friends" – in my life and slipped into my old ways. I no longer heard what my husband was telling me, but instead started to hear whispers from those now around me, that he did not love me. I was being told on a regular basis that I would be better off without him in my life. This fed into my fears, it validated them and made them true in my mind.

I can remember talking with my new "friends" about how I felt torn between what my past was telling me and what my husband's responses were. I told them how he would tell me that I needed to listen to him and stop allowing my past to influence how I was living my current life. Instead of telling me that he was right, which he was, I was being told that he was controlling me and that I should make him leave.

I started to really push him away because now my thoughts of him hurting me were validated and, since I was still weak mentally from all the pain I had endured,

I believed those people over him. It got so bad that I can remember the day that almost ended us.

I remember taking a shower and telling myself that I had to tell him the truth. I had to tell him no matter how bad it would hurt him, because I owed him that. He did not deserve to be hurt by me or my past anymore. It was no longer me fearing him hurting me, the fear turned into me fearing him leaving because of what I had done to hurt him. I could not believe I allowed myself to get so caught up in what other people were saying, people who had no idea what they were even talking about. All I knew in that moment was that I was sick of feeling torn between my past, my new "friends", and what I wanted – my husband. I needed to make the madness stop once and for all.

I sat on our bed as he was getting dressed and told him how I had been being influenced and how I did not think he loved me or that I could trust him. I will never forget the look in his eyes when the words came out of my mouth. I had never seen him so angry as he started to get all his clothes out of our dresser and was telling me he could not stay there with me if I was going to continue to go down this path and not believe him when he told me he loved me. He could not handle the pain I was bringing into his life.

I begged him with tears crashing down to stay. In the moment I decided to tell him he should leave, I quickly realized that I could not allow that to happen. My soul started to scream at me to fix this and to not let him walk out that door. I promised him I would start to listen and stop allowing other people to influence me. Thankfully, he stopped packing and put his clothes back in the drawers and told me that he was not sure how to process what had happened and that he would need time, but that his love for me was so strong that he was not leaving.

The fear of love that I had was something I needed to figure out and fast because I knew he could not handle anymore from me. If something else happened that threatened our marriage due to my fears, I would lose him. So, I started to look inward to figure out why I was so resistant to his love and why I kept sabotaging my life.

I started by writing down my thoughts and stories of my past. I started to notice a common theme across all the bad things and relationships I had been in, both with men and friendships. The common theme ended up being that I did not know who I was. I had spent my entire adult life searching for love and acceptance, but the bottom line was that I did not love and accept myself. I did not forgive myself for making bad choices and was convinced that I only deserved hardship. I was negative all the time and was constantly judging others, just so I could feel better about myself. I turned into a monster, someone who destroyed everything good that came into my life in fear of what the people around me at the time would think. I never listened to myself, and I certainly did not know how to stand up for what I felt was right.

I decided to dig deep and figure out what my values were and to figure out what I wanted when it came to my life and love. My top core value quickly came to me, and it is second chances. In figuring this out, I realized that I never gave myself a second chance. I never forgave myself in order to allow second chances into my life.

One day, as I was sitting with my thoughts and my recent realization, I chose to forgive myself and give myself a second chance. The first thing I needed to do was allow myself to accept my husband's love and to allow myself to trust him completely. I needed to stop waiting for him to hurt me like everyone had done in the past. I deserved his love and he deserved to have the best version of me loving and trusting him back.

I allowed myself to fully open my heart to him and trust him completely. This was not an easy decision for me to make, but I knew in my heart that it was right. In making the decision, our marriage grew even stronger. I can remember telling him that I fully trusted him and accepted his love. He was so happy and grateful that I finally saw our marriage the way he did. Yes, it was risky, considering my track record when it came to relationships, but something told me I needed to let go of the past and really see what was right in front of me. I am so grateful that I made this choice.

It took a while for him to trust me again, but I knew it was worth the wait. As I was growing as a person, he still held my hand. We made a promise to always communicate with each other, no matter what was going on in our lives. I went to him when things started to get a bit over my head, and he would talk to me and help me figure out how to fully trust myself to make the right choices. Even though

I had hurt him, and his trust was still not fully bloomed, he never once turned his back on me. He did not treat me differently and to this day does not throw it back in my face. Our love grew and his trust for me came back over time. He brought the good out of me and together we kissed the old me goodbye.

As I write this chapter, it is our four-year anniversary and, let me tell you, I never thought I would get married, let alone stay married for four years. Especially not to a man who absolutely loves me. I see love differently than I used to. It does not have to be a struggle and I do not always have to be the one making the good things happen. Fighting does not have to be an everyday occurrence either. I am allowed to be myself in all situations and never feel judged. I know it is cliché, but love is not supposed to hurt. It is supposed to feel good. Love is meant to fill our hearts and make us smile and not just with our faces, but with our souls too.

In finding the love of my life, I learned that not every person is going to hurt me. There are people in this world who will love me for who I am. Opening my heart to my husband was one of the hardest things I have done in my life, but it has had the most amazing rewards. To this day, when he is in the room with me I feel electricity, and when he is not here with me I miss him like I have not seen him in years. He has never once lied to me and has always had my back. True love does exist; there are good people in the world who will pick us up and love us completely.

Even when we are stuck in self sabotage, like I was a

few years ago, we can have love in our lives. It may not be easy to see at first, but it does exist. Once I let go of trying to please everyone around me and figured out who I am and what I want in life, the doors started to open, and love was showered over me.

Because of his love, I was finally able to see the world the way I had imagined it in the past. A world with a true partner and no longer me fighting for peace. I no longer need to worry about what tomorrow will bring because I know, with him by my side, everything will be okay. This is not a fairy tale or a dream I had. This is real life and, even when it is messy, as it always seems to get from time to time, we get through it together.

As I said throughout my story, this was not easy, and it took a lot for me to be able to trust my husband. The point is that true love is possible, and it is out there for all of us. Even when we feel broken and lost, there is someone out there waiting for us. Someone waiting to love us who will accept us as we are in any moment. Someone who will allow us to feel our pain and not judge us. This person will hold us when we are down and understand when we need a moment to ourselves. They will not hurt us, but lift us up when others do. Remember, we all deserve a second chance, and we do not have to live our lives hurting and crying more than we are laughing. We just have to be open to let the good things into our lives and that includes love.

Use this space to journal:

Journal questions:

1. How do you feel after reading this chapter?
2. The turning point was when I figured out what my personal values were, not what others had told me. What are your top personal values?

_____

_____

_____

_____

_____

_____

_____

_____

_____

_____

_____

_____

_____

_____

_____

That's True Freedom and I Love It

Caron Kipping

I vividly remember sitting in the bedroom in the nurses' accommodation, thinking, "It's okay, it won't always be like this, one day we won't be together anymore, and it will be okay. I don't know when that will be, but I know it will happen." There was nothing particular that triggered that statement – nobody to say it to, but myself. It was just a general feeling, a recognition that it would be okay someday, a comfort that one day this constant feeling of sadness and inevitability would stop. I seemed to somehow recognise that this wasn't okay. I couldn't describe what wasn't okay to anyone, even if they had asked me at the time, but it was sort of a premonition that this relationship wouldn't last, that it would come to an end at some point in the future. I had no idea when or how, but I just knew deep down that it would. I don't even remember how the general day-to-day sadness and sense of inevitability started; it must have crept in after the initial buzz of having a boyfriend who showed me attention for longer than a couple of weeks had worn off. I didn't have any sense of enjoyment anymore – I had lost my friends, any zest I had for life, any confidence I had (which wasn't much to start with), and each day seemed to merge into the next. I never looked forward to anything anymore, everything became stressful, everything seemed negative, and I never did anything I wanted anymore.

Fast forward ten years and that day when everything was going to change had come – yes, it took a while! I had tried before and failed because I hadn't planned it properly or thought it through. He would find me, put on the guilt treatment, plead, beg, cry, talk 'at me' for hours – no discussion, no listening, just hours of justifying his behaviour and giving me endless reasons why we needed to stick together. I gave in because I was just so blooming exhausted I would have agreed to anything. I just wanted him to shut up, stop talking, leave me alone and let me go to sleep. Of course, each time it was actually worse after I went back – he was more clingy, more paranoid, more insecure than ever, so the control became worse. He wouldn't dare let me leave again – he couldn't cope on his own and the thought that I might be able to frightened him.

This is a common pattern with people who try to leave abusive relationships – the average number of attempts before leaving for good is eight times. It took me three times, but there were years in between each one, until I knew enough was enough. Each time my confidence was knocked, I began to believe that I wasn't strong enough, that it would be okay if we got married, if we moved to a bigger house, if we had a baby. Of course, it didn't help – it simply tethered me to him even more.

This last time, however, was different. I wasn't going

to fall for any of it. I was ready for the tears, the threats, the excuses, the lies, and I knew they weren't going to work this time. I was strong enough to handle it, I wasn't going to give in this time, no matter what. The resentment, anger, frustration that had festered inside of me for years was bubbling to the surface and I knew I had to get out. I couldn't stand to look at him anymore, never mind speak to him, and he began to see that, which often made him angry. In my head I had emotionally disconnected from him, but I also knew I had to make it as easy for myself as possible. If I didn't leave soon, it was going to get worse anyway, so it was 'make or break'. I planned it. I confided in a couple of friends – the only ones I had left. I went as far away as I could – so he couldn't physically reach me – to family who could support me. I hadn't thought through anything more than that – just how to get from home to the train station, with everything in a bag, and off I went. A quick call to double-check my family were going to be in and I was on my way. I don't know what I would have done if they hadn't been! It was the scariest but most decisive thing I had ever done and there was no going back!

So up I rocked, at Waverley station in Edinburgh, shaking like a leaf, not knowing how to explain what had just happened. I didn't talk much while I was there – I didn't know how to explain just how bad things had become. If you say, "He doesn't like me wearing makeup," it doesn't sound like anything serious enough to warrant ending your marriage, but I felt suffocated, like I had lost 'me'. I went for walks by the sea, wondering what was going to happen next, but not wanting to think about that. I just wanted to stay in my little 'escape bubble' for a while.

I did other things to keep myself strong. I threw away my contraceptive pills – no need for those anymore! I didn't answer his calls often, and when I did, I made it very clear I wasn't coming home to him, and he knew I meant it. I realised straight away how nice it was not to have him around and already I loved that feeling. I remember saying to myself, "I won't have to do xx anymore." I would make a mental list of all the things I wouldn't have to do or say anymore. No more having to write 'I love you' on cards when I didn't mean it. No more giving in to bullying, sulking and threats. There was a lot on the list, and it felt so good knowing that I didn't have to do any of those things anymore.

I tried to explain it to my family, but it didn't really make sense to me, let alone them. I had a feeling they didn't like him, but nobody had ever said that to me directly and there hadn't been any physical abuse, so it must have been difficult for them to understand. How can you explain how bad someone makes you feel when it is just 'he doesn't like me wearing makeup' or 'we don't go out', it really doesn't seem that bad. When you understand the reasons why you don't go out and understand the jealousy, false accusations, criticism and name-calling that come with simply wearing a little makeup, then perhaps you can appreciate how difficult it is to be in a relationship with someone like this. It's not just about makeup, it's about everything you do, everything you say, everything you are. When it is constant, when you can never do anything right, when you feel cheap and worthless because the person you are with makes you feel like that, it's degrading, it's debilitating and exhausting. Even though I had only just left him, the sense of knowing that I never had to do any of those things again or justify myself to him again was exhilarating.

I was free and there was no way I was going back to being that person again – the one who put up with it, who stayed silent because it was easier, who protected him because I felt embarrassed and ashamed of his behaviour, because I didn't know how to make him stop. I knew I wasn't the problem – I had been made to believe I was, but deep down I think I always knew he was the problem. To be honest, now I was out, I didn't care what he thought or what anyone else thought, I wasn't going to live my life for anyone else again – ever!

Needless to say, this wasn't as easy as I thought it was going to be! In my head I thought we could be perfectly amicable, able to co-parent, able to accept that we both needed to move on. We were going to be the perfect couple who managed to 'get over it', to put our child first, but no, of course that was never going to be the case. How naïve was I?! The next few years were a rollercoaster, there were highs and lots of lows, but even though things were really tough (understatement of the century), I always knew leaving had still been the right thing to do. NO matter how bad things were, how stressful they were, it was still better than living how I had been living for all those years. Nothing was ever going to get me to go back.

I had just been existing before, not even living. There had been no fun, no enjoyment, no nothing for years. As a result of leaving him, I lost even more, I lost almost everything. I had no money, was up to my eyes in debt, stressed to the max about how I was going to get out of this mess and yet still it was better. Friends that I had lost touch with rallied round, offering me a place to stay, buying me clothes, buying me food, giving me their shoulder to cry on and telling me it would be okay. They made me laugh again, helped me try to see the funny side of a really bad situation, reminded me that I was, in actual fact, a good person, and helped me see that things could get better. I got closer with my family again, they helped me and, as things continued to be difficult, they could get some sense of what my life had really been like before I left. I started to see the light at the end of the tunnel.

Some days I would feel strong – other days I would wonder how on earth I could have let things get to this point. I came from a good family, I had a good education, a good career, but my personal life was disastrous. I felt lonely, afraid of the future, but kept reminding myself that I had done nothing wrong. I let go of the guilt that was eating me up and started to feel stronger again. I tested things out, told myself I would never allow myself to be manipulated again and anyone who was in a relationship with me in future either liked me as I was, or they could take a running jump!

I was lucky that I met my husband fairly soon after my abusive relationship. Looking back, I should never have jumped into another relationship so quickly – I was badly wounded, had no idea about warning signs of abuse, I could have ended up in another similar relationship and another nightmare! I was just lucky that one of the good ones found me. He was kind, looked after me, gave me freedom without question, trusted me right from the beginning and gradually we built a life together. I was honest about my previous relationship, and he never judged me or blamed me. I gave him little tests at the beginning, such as seeing how he would react if I mentioned a girl's night out – 'Have a good time,' he said, that was it. He bought me nice clothes, encouraged me to do things that made me feel better and gradually built me up from the shell that had been left.

My ex was still festering in the background, but I learnt ways of dealing with him. I worked out that ignoring him worked best – trying to challenge him or expecting him to be reasonable never worked. He loved having the upper hand at any and every opportunity. I learnt to always look my best if I had to see him, even if I didn't feel it – it felt like I was wearing a suit of armour. If I felt good, I felt more confident, and it was my little way of showing him that no matter what he had tried to do to me, I was winning, not him. I was still standing, still showing up, still thriving.

As I became stronger and I had more positive things to fill up my life, I became more confident. I learnt to let go of the guilt for how things had worked out, for how it had affected the children and the wider family. I hadn't caused any of this. I knew I wasn't the problem, so therefore I made a conscious decision that I wasn't going to bear the weight of that guilt and responsibility anymore. When he was being difficult, instead of confronting him and getting caught up in a battle, I would let it go. I wouldn't ask him for anything – I didn't want to give him any opportunity to say 'no', just because he felt like it. If he tried to blame me for something, I would simply put the phone down or flip it round and put the focus back on him. He didn't know what to do with that – no fuel for his fire, no arguments, no drama. It was a turning point.

After a few years I had a 'sliding doors' moment. I was at work when the CEO of my local charity came to give us a talk about domestic abuse. Obviously, I could connect with everything she said, especially when she explained about how the women felt. She asked for volunteers at the end of her talk – she didn't explain what it would involve but said we could go along to a volunteers evening if we were interested. Straight away, my ears pricked up. I didn't know how I could help, but I knew I had to go. There would be people there like me, who understood, who I could help.

So, I went along and there were a group of about ten people in the front living room at one of the refuge homes. We all had to say why we wanted to volunteer. I was really nervous. 'What if they don't want me? What if they think I am 'damaged goods', and my story is too bad?' Of course, I know now that actually there are many women who have experienced many things much worse than me, but at the time I thought I was the only one who had experienced such awful things.

Anyway, luckily, they did decide to take me on! I offered to volunteer for a couple of hours, once a week, because my children were still young and, also, I was a bit unsure about whether I would be able to cope with what they were going to ask me to do. To start with, I was just making up beds after families had left the refuge home and helping collect families who were coming in, but I knew I loved it already. I felt a sense of purpose. I knew that even if it was just making up a bed, it was doing something good, something worthwhile, helping someone who felt as desperate as I had felt a few years previously. I was worried that I wouldn't be able to let go of some of the worry about the families we were helping, and it took time. I used to think about them even when I wasn't there, but the staff were really supportive, and it was a lovely, fun and kind place to be.

I was already working in a caring profession, but it had never been a vocation. It had been a job that I enjoyed, that I was proud of, but this felt different. The refuge then asked me if I wanted a job. I deliberated for about five minutes then said yes! I had to take a bit of a pay cut, to leave the security of the NHS, but I knew it was now or never. I loved it! I woke up every day excited about going to work – each day was different, there were definitely challenges, but it was heart-warming to get cuddles from the children in our care and to see the women recovering and finding themselves again. Funnily enough, over the years, a few of my NHS colleagues have joined me at the charity and we have always said never a day has gone by that we haven't woken up and looked forward to going to work.

Yes, some days are tough – the challenges that come with working for a small charity are difficult. The challenges that come with hearing some of the stories we listen to are tough, but above all, we know we make a difference. The passion shines through from every single person in our teams who go above and beyond to support these vulnerable women, men and children who feel lost, hopeless and very often terrified.

I have now worked in various roles over the fourteen years I have been there, after training as one of the first IDVAs in the UK. An IDVA is an Independent Domestic Violence Advocate – someone who specialises in supporting people experiencing domestic abuse. We speak up when they feel like they aren't being heard, we try our best to get them the help they need and that they are entitled to and we help them understand that they don't have to put up with a relationship where your needs are last, where you are made to feel worthless, where you are afraid.

For a while I worked with women whose abusers have been sentenced to perpetrator programmes. Most of that time was spent trying to manage their expectations and keep them safe, because we all want to see the best in people and to hope that they can change, but often that change is just too difficult. For many of these men, these attitudes and behaviours are so deeply entrenched that they simply can't change, even if they wanted to – which lots of them don't. I also worked with young mums in abusive relationships, many of whom would have a baby with their abuser, hoping to have this happy little family unit to cement their 'love', only to realise that having a baby would make an already horrendous situation even worse; that it wasn't actually love, it was control and that they would be tied together with their abuser forever.

I have supported some of the most challenging and complex clients, who have on occasion brought me to tears with frustration because they can't get the help they so badly need or because others simply don't 'get it'. I have cried with frustration at the hours spent fundraising to keep services alive (that actually do save lives) when those with the power to finance those services have turned their back. How is this kind of work and support even charitable in the first place??

I have trained social workers, housing officers, teachers, therapists, solicitors and the general public – trying to get them to understand why it is so hard to leave, to respond better and maybe think about how they can do better, be better, how they can help. I have done my fair share of fundraising – ran my first 5k with no training on the hottest day of the year (thought I was going to die from heatstroke), shaken many a bucket in the pouring rain, but had a barrel of laughs while doing it.

My work at The Dash Charity has certainly never been dull but, as with many other local charities, life working in this field is a roller coaster too. It makes you adaptable, it helps you learn lots of skills and and it's always interesting, but a few years ago I had to take a back seat from the frontline work and move into the fundraising team full-time. I hated it at first – I have always been a 'people person', so sitting at a desk writing grant application after grant application and getting knocked back quite a few times was soul destroying. I have never been one to want a desk job – I love talking with actual people, so I continued in my training role, too, and started working closely with our new patron Sara Davison.

Sara is one of the UK's leading divorce coaches. Like many people, I had never heard of divorce coaching before and started to learn more about it. I loved the way coaching offers practical tools and strategies to help people in need and started to see how this could help the people that Dash simply couldn't help. I was listening to calls on the helpline from people desperate for help – they were having a terrible divorce, but it wasn't domestic abuse, they were locked in conflict with an ex over child contact arrangements, but the risk wasn't high enough or they were out of area, so we had to signpost them on to other services.

It made me wonder who these people went to for help. Their solicitor who would charge them a hefty fee for a telephone call but who wouldn't necessarily know how to support them emotionally? Would they be forced to struggle alone like I did, or go to services who didn't understand the risk of domestic abuse? Or services who don't appreciate that abuse doesn't just end when your case is closed? When you have a baby together you are tied for life – there will be issues that crop up from time to time over years. Your ex may start harassing you (but not enough that police get involved), your ex may continue to argue over every little issue (and after several years that can become very tiresome) or you may simply be exhausted and need to rediscover who the heck you are after years of dealing with your ex's crap! Setting out on the divorce journey against an abusive ex is scary. If you don't know what you are doing, what your rights are or how to take that control back, it can be a dangerous and difficult experience. If you make the wrong choices these can affect you for years, as I know, having learnt the hard way. I didn't want anyone else to make the same mistakes I did.

The way you coach a client is essentially what I had been doing for years as an IDVA, it was just called something else. It was a different client base, but I knew I could make a difference this way too. I signed up for Sara's course and learnt some more strategies and tools to add to what I already had and set up my business. I wasn't sure if there would be a demand for what I did, but there weren't any major setting up costs, so again it was a 'now or never' moment. I didn't want to regret anything years later. I didn't want to say to myself I could have done something, but I was too scared, so I put myself out there. The Dash team were brilliant – they recognised the value of my business and how it could complement what they do. Professional contacts were pleased they could finally signpost to someone who understood the risks completely and who had the experience and skills to support their clients. My support makes the job of the solicitor easier – helping clients focus better, think more clearly, have confidence to move forward. I have met loads of other professionals too in this new business world – divorce consultants, financial planners, mediators, even house movers (never knew there was such a thing) and therapists. It is wonderful to be part of a community of divorce coaches and professionals all focused on helping clients move on to bigger and better things. I love the positivity that comes with coaching – yes, things are tough, things don't always go to plan, but no matter what, my clients know they are not facing things alone.

I now get to help clients all over the world, am regularly asked to comment in the media and I have the flexibility to support clients for as long as they need me. Several of my clients are now in happy relationships after suffering abuse for years and some are happily single and enjoying the freedom they have found. I regularly get feedback from them and comments like, "I couldn't have done this without you," or, "I never thought this was possible," and for me, that is the biggest buzz of all.

I have recently had an article published in *The Independent* and wrote my book *Recognition to Recovery – How to leave your abusive ex behind for good!* It took me a while to write it – I have always loved writing, but I didn't want it to be just another survivor story. To be honest, I tried writing my story at first, but I couldn't do it. I have blocked out some of what happened and, also, I wanted my book to be more inspirational and about positive change. I didn't want it to be about me. I shared some real-life examples from women I have supported over the years, to show people that what they have experienced or how they feel is not unusual. I wanted them to understand how they got into these relationships and, importantly, to show them how to recover. I used the strategies I learnt in my personal experience and those I learnt as a professional to create a huge toolkit to get people through those early days and right through to longer-term recovery.

Simple tips such as changing your routines can really change your mindset and get you refocused on life now compared to how it was. If you always went to the same supermarket with your ex, going to a new one, pushing the trolley when you weren't previously allowed to because you were 'clearly too stupid to do so' then choosing what food you want to eat with no worries about it being thrown across the kitchen can help remind you of why you left and why it is good now. Not perfect, but good right now, and that's a stepping stone to where you want to be eventually. Rome wasn't built in a day!

I was worried about what other people would think when the book was published – would they criticise it, would it be helpful or was that my ego talking?! I needn't have worried – the feedback has been amazing from professionals and the public and I am so glad I took the plunge. That's one thing ticked off my bucket list – again, a 'do it or regret it' moment. The reviews have been amazing and women from all different backgrounds and at different stages have told me how much the book has helped them. I can now proudly say I am a published author!

I always say, "Domestic abuse doesn't have to define you – it shapes you, but it isn't who you are." You can be anything you want to be.

Just because you don't feel strong, doesn't mean you aren't strong. You don't feel strong because of how someone has made you feel. You ARE strong – you have to be to put up with abuse; this strength will help you at every step. You ARE kind too – if you weren't you wouldn't have given your ex so many chances or made so many excuses for them. Don't let your experiences put you off and don't let it stop you from being who you are. Find true happiness within you – you don't need anyone else to give you that. If you are putting all the responsibility for your happiness in someone else's hands, it leaves you very vulnerable and also a prime target for manipulation from those who have the desire to control you. True happiness needs to come from within – see your strengths, find those positive qualities that you possess, believe yourself when you say you are good enough and don't wait for the perfect time to change your situation if it isn't serving you as it should. There will never be a perfect time.

I never felt strong when I was in my abusive relationship but, since I left my ex, I have achieved so much more than I ever thought I could. I have met the prime minister, taken part in a BAFTA-nominated documentary 'Behind Closed Doors' and met so many inspiring and amazing people that have helped me find my voice again. I will look back on my life and be proud of who I am and what I have done. I am no longer ashamed of my story – it has made me who I am, as corny as that seems. While I would never want to go through it again or wish anyone else to, I don't think I would have achieved so much without it – it gave me a career I love and helps me appreciate the small things every day. I wear what I want, speak up when I want to, I have fun when I can, and I choose who I want in my life. I don't get stressed about much these days, as I know whatever happens I will be okay. That's true freedom and I love it!

Don't ever settle for less than you deserve. Get support, get out safely and then spend every day working on your recovery and making the most of each day – you won't regret it!

Use this space to journal:

Journal questions:

1. What would you like your future to look like?
2. Have you got dreams you always wanted to achieve?
3. Have you got places you want to visit, people you want to rekindle relationships with, fun things you want to do again?
4. What can you do to get there?
5. The world really can be your oyster if you set your mind to it!

_____

_____

_____

_____

_____

_____

_____

_____

_____

_____

_____

_____

_____

_____

_____

_____

_____

_____

_____

_____

_____

_____

_____

_____

_____

_____

_____

_____

_____

_____

_____

_____

_____

The Energy Shift That Will Transform Your Whole World

Vicki Chisholm

The Energy Shift.

There was one session that changed my life! It was the door that opened and brought me to where I am today… and I will very proudly say, this place I'm in right now is the most beautiful place of all.

Within approximately thirty minutes of my coaching session with Jen, she had helped me see a bigger vision that I didn't think was possible. Within forty-eight hours of that session, I woke up and felt different. I felt lighter, more empowered, and ready to OWN MY LIFE.

I never realised how three words, 'Emotional Freedom Technique' would change my life. It's so much more than just these three words, though. The name of this phenomenal technique is just the start. I was twenty-one when I was first introduced to EFT with my counsellor, but I was not willing to try it. So, roll on ten years, I'm asked to do it again. I waited until I was at breaking point, desperate to create some change, and feel like a 'normal' human being. To accept the offer of EFT.

Emotional Freedom Technique (EFT) is energy psychology that uses the meridian points on the body (Chinese culture acupressure) to release stuck and stagnant energy, and rewire the brainwaves of emotional reactivity. Every memory you have has an emotion attached to it, so by tapping on the meridian points you can release emotionally charged memories from your system, in turn bringing you to a foundation of inner peace. What I found with EFT is that it reduced pain in my body too, it reduced my stress levels, and it could take me from having a full-blown crying frenzy to calm in a matter of moments. It really was like a magic pill!

EFT sounds SUPER crazy, but it works! Literally just by tapping on your face you can change how you feel!

I'd spent many years of my life being told that anything holistic was a load of rubbish, but there was this small part of me that was intrigued by it. I loved the metaphysical world. But, at the same time, I was petrified of it. The unknown, being out of my comfort zone, fearing the worst and not having any way of controlling what would/could happen was holding me back. With that on top of the ridicule, I was so torn. How could I lean into this and fully believe in it when everyone around me was filled with negativity? Any time I wanted to venture into it, learn more, allow my curiosity to flow, I was shot down.

The relationship I had spent twelve years in was crushing my soul. Controlling, lifeless and, well, I was an empty shell. I would go food shopping and get phone calls as to why I was taking so long. I would be doing it all, with very little support and, no matter what, everything was my fault.

Nothing I ever did was ever enough.

Taking time for myself was not something that happened or worth the aggro.

All I knew was work, kids, housework and work. Simply to live a peaceful life.

One of my friends was a psychotherapist and one day she said to me, "Vicki who are you?"

This was a tough question. I started saying, "Well, I'm a mum, cook, cleaner and hard worker."

She stopped me there and said, "Vicki, that's what you do. Who are you?"

I burst into tears. I didn't know what to say. I got frustrated because I didn't know how to answer this question.

As time passed, prior to my sessions with Jen, I would often find myself looking in the mirror and not even recognising the person staring back at me.

Jen was my business coach for my virtual assistant business. I booked this particular coaching session one evening to go through some work I had been doing for a client – I really needed some validation and support. The client was claiming I had got it wrong and I wasn't getting it. I showed Jen the communication and the work I had completed. I was so confused and couldn't see past my emotions of fear of failure. I just had tears streaming down my face, tears of fear, tears of panic. My thoughts were very negative and in those moments all I kept thinking was how could I get this so wrong, and why can't I find the mistake that I've made?

Jen sat up and said, "Vicki, what exactly do you think you have done wrong here?"

I said, "I don't know, that's why I'm so upset because I don't know how to fix it. I believe I've done everything I could have and should have but it's still not right, what have I missed, Jen?"

Jen looked at me and said, "Vicki, darling, you have done everything that you should have and could have, the client is not clearly communicating, which is her problem. You have done EXACTLY what she asked. Vicki, on a scale of nought to ten, where is your self-worth right now?" Ouch, ouch, ouch. I sobbed even more than I had done previously. I was a mess. My self-worth... I didn't even know what that meant.

So, as I sat there in this moment, sobbing my heart out, feeling like the most useless woman on the planet, totally broken, Jen offered me a tissue and some compassion, and she said, "Vicki, would you be willing to humour me and try some tapping?" I nodded my head through the sobbing.

In the moment before this, Jen knew what was going on for me at home, even though she had never said it, she knew. I trusted Jen and, because of this, I allowed her to guide me through my first ever EFT tapping experience.

As I sat there and sobbed and just felt completely distraught, Jen asked me to tap with her. We tapped on the side of the hands, and she asked me to repeat after her. At first, I found it hard to repeat the words, and some words she said I couldn't even say.

The set-up phrase goes like this:

Tapping on the side of the hand and repeat: "Even though, I am feeling completely worthless right now and I can't seem to do anything right… I deeply and completely love and accept myself anyway."

We had to repeat that three times. We then moved on to the other tapping points. Eyebrow, side of the eye, under the eye, under the nose, collarbone, etc… these meridian points seemed to do something. I was feeling less and less distressed. It was like I was given this magic wand. I was feeling better and better.

I wasn't ever good at showing emotion. In fact, I would do anything I could to hide and suppress it, so when this avalanche of emotion overpowered me, I knew I was in a difficult space.

The session progressed, more tears flowed and flowed. But how they felt changed.

I ended the contract with the client and walked away. My inner peace was worth more.

The strangest part of this experience was, as I was going home, I still had tears streaming down my face and I was really exhausted at this point. The reality that I had no self-belief, no self-worth, no confidence, no real support and was an empty shell consumed me… it was all too much. I was in a mess. The reality was I was sitting crying because

176

I couldn't 'fix' a problem that wasn't even my problem to 'fix'! I was sooo lost... I didn't even know who I was, or how to find me.

An abusive relationship and years of trauma had taken its toll. And I just thought to myself, "Who the hell am I?!"

I went in and went straight to bed. I was exhausted.

The next day, I woke up and something felt 'off', different and confused. It was like I felt lighter, but I was still 'fat', I hadn't lost any physical weight. So, this just made me sound even crazier! I texted Jen and said, "I feel really weird. Is this normal??" She confirmed that yes, EFT can in fact make you feel lighter, it's one of the benefits.

It had been a few days since my session with Jen, and another argument broke out, this time because I worked too much. I just remember looking at him and saying, "Well, what else should I be doing?"

He said, "Come and chill with me." (You know what that means!)

And I just said, "No, I don't want to. I don't want to be in this relationship anymore with the way things are." I couldn't cope with endless accusations every time I had a business meeting, or the way he treated the kids so I wouldn't ask him for help or the way that I was left to deal with everything on my own, plus meet his expectations too.

I couldn't believe those words had come out of my mouth! I was suddenly strong... from just ONE session! I was hooked, I wanted to see where this could take me.

I gave six months' notice in my relationship: if the change didn't happen, I would be gone. Needless to say, things went from bad to worse. So off I went five months later to embark on a journey that was all about reclaiming my life.

Don't get me wrong, it wasn't a picnic. I had to rehome myself and three children, attempt to co-parent with my ex-partner and so much more. But, for over a year, I managed and found a way to continue running my business and look after my children.

2016 came flying around the corner and things still hadn't changed much; in fact, the same old stories just kept on repeating, with varying degrees of seriousness. But it was also very liberating, as I had my first ever child-free weekend… and then another one, and another one. I should have been focusing on business or household stuff like I always had, but I couldn't… I couldn't do the mundane when I was child free. I was ready to live! I was ready to go and explore a little bit and see what the world had on offer.

I started going out with friends, I took myself off to run on a beach – simply because I could. I joined a gym and would sit in the hot tub. All these wonderful things. The months passed and I didn't want to stop living. I couldn't believe I could have this freedom – it was weird, and I was constantly worrying about the kids, but I also needed this time to just be me. I sat with my friend and was telling her about the adventures I was having and also questioning my sanity. Her words to me were, "Vicki, if you take a deprived child to a sweet shop for the first time and let them have what they want, do you think they are going to dip their toe in and have a sneak peek or do you think they are going to dive in and refuse to come back out?" Ah! Okay... so, this need for enjoyment of life and freedom was because in all my adult years I had never had it.

July 2016, though, this was a game changer!

I was noticing how tired I was becoming, chronic fatigue and fibromyalgia flare ups, plus anxiety and depression, a business to run, staff to manage, clients and three kids under the age of eleven to look after... I was flaking. One day, my phone went. I answered and it was an urgent call to go to the school and collect my daughter for emergency care at the hospital. So off I went, petrified of what may have been. I got her to the hospital, her symptoms were those of a heart attack and we had to wait for test results with eight weeks of no exercise.

This was the crunch point. I was done. I couldn't take any more.

I quit, shut down my business, walked away from everything and took the time I needed to focus on my family, but more importantly manage my own health. I was burnt out.

After a few months of resting and trying to get back on my feet, I went through sixteen weeks of psychotherapy. It hadn't changed how I felt, I felt the same after sixteen weeks of psychotherapy as I did when I walked in! I was devastated and part of me felt my life was over.

This was until I had an epiphany. If tapping could

179

help me back then... then it can help me now. So off I went to contact those I knew in the field and enquired about training. A family friend was one of the ladies on my contact list, and Maria sent me the details of the most incredible mentors I could have ever crossed paths with: Ranjana Appoo and her husband Eddie Appoo. Wow, the admiration I have for these two is beyond anything I have ever experienced.

Ranjana became a woman who was so much more than just a mentor for me; she showed me the truth of all that I was, even when I didn't believe her. As I progressed and moved forward, I was able to look back and reflect on all that she had done for me, simply by sharing her wisdom, kindness and, most of all, unconditional love. The golden nuggets of wisdom Ranjana and Eddie would share with me not only challenged me out of my own crazy mind, but helped me see beyond the scars and wounds I was holding.

It all started in February 2017... my journey to personal peace began.

I sat in the corner of the room on my first training weekend. The far corner, with a 'don't look at me, don't talk to me, don't expect anything from me' attitude. I wanted to run, I wanted to hide, but more importantly the only thing keeping me sitting there was I wanted change; I wanted incredible transformation. I was done with the life I had lived. I was ready to face this fear and change my life.

I learnt so much in that weekend, and when I look back now, I am so blessed that I was given that opportunity to learn, grow and evolve with the powerhouse trainers that I had. They were so much more than just trainers, they were heart-led souls whose passion is to open love and truth to the wider world/community.

As mentioned at the beginning of this chapter, I was first introduced to EFT when I was twenty-one, but when my counsellor said to me, "Will you humour me and simply tap on your face to move through this emotion?" I said no. My ego and pride were very prominent then.

My words to her at that time were: "If you think for one minute I'm going to sit here and tap on my face and make myself look like an idiot you've got another thing coming." Now I could kick myself! If I had said yes to EFT at the age of twenty-one, the rest of my twenties would have been very different. But this is what makes this journey so unique. I've learnt a lesson with this. Say yes to yourself, allow yourself to do the things that feel uncomfortable. It could just change your life!

As I progressed through levels one and two of EFT training, my mentor said, "Vicki, you are going to make a fabulous practitioner one day."

This was a shock to my system. I said, "No I won't, I have zero intentions of working with people, I just want to help myself feel better right now. My girls deserve better than this mess that was staring back at me through the mirror."

My mentor nodded and said, "But Vicki, to qualify you will be required to undertake case studies."

In that moment I had a choice: continue to learn to

help myself and others or walk away. Well, the training I did helped me so much I decided to stay on and do the case studies.

This was an interesting viewpoint altogether. I was so resistant to change. I was afraid of losing control, I had such a negative, withdrawn and unworthy attitude about myself. My biggest fear of all was how on earth could I help other people when I am in such a bad place myself, emotionally, mentally and physically? This was my challenge, and I somehow had to overcome this. I'm going to come back to this a bit later, but for now I want to share some amazing insights with you!

After taking on my journey with EFT, I decided to embark on another journey... the journey of Reiki! Energy healing from the inside out! Imagine being in science in school and you put your hands in front of you like a ball shape and you pull them apart and then back together again. Do you remember that? The physics class where they briefly explain energy, atoms and particles... well, you may never consider that class the same again after reading this.

Reiki is that energy you hold in your hands. That when you pull your hands apart and push them closer together you can start to feel the energy build. Reiki is universal energy, which once attuned to you can channel at a much higher frequency.

Reiki is just like the wind, you can feel it and sense it, but you can't see it, smell it, touch it or taste it. But you still know it's there. I've always been drawn to this woo-woo stuff, even if there were parts of me that were afraid of the power that they may have. Part of me just knew I had to learn how to channel this healing energy to help me clear the energies in my body that I could not see!

So, armed with EFT and Reiki, it was time to for me to get this show on the road. I started offering combined sessions and I was blown away! This was when I decided it was time to get my business head back on and start sharing my gifts with the world.

I started my journey with shifting energy in 2017 and, by the end of 2019, I was free from fibromyalgia, chronic fatigue, anxiety, depression and PTSD. I had made the impossible more than possible. Doctors had told me I would never find a cure, only coping mechanisms. (Of course, medical advice should never be ignored, so please don't replace anything just by reading this journey. Do your research... but more importantly listen to your intuition.)

Throughout the two years of 2017-2019, I had opened the door to start helping people again. This may not seem like such a big thing, but for me this was going against everything I was standing for in that moment. I didn't want to work with anyone, I didn't want to be someone who others needed – my goodness, I had enough on my plate. I was still healing my own mind and heart, the thought of helping others petrified me, as this would mean letting people in. This would mean I would have to be seen and this would mean I would have to really pull my shit together, but I was nothing but a nervous mess of broken pieces that needed to be put back together again.

As time passed and I carried out the case studies, I wholeheartedly believed that I wasn't good enough, strong enough or worthy to be doing this work. Until the results spoke for themselves. Suddenly, there I was, changing lives, whilst still figuring out the healing in my own life. This was when shifting energy became an obsession. In 2018, I started opening the doors to be back in business again and this was when I also decided to become a transformational coach. I got certified as a coach and completed Reiki Master Trainer Certification as well as an accredited advanced EFT practitioner.

I was told by Ranjana once, it's not a one-off tool. It's just as important as brushing your teeth twice a day! It's a lifestyle choice.

One of the nuggets that Ranjana used to help me move through my own stuckness was this: "What you resist will persist. Stay there if you choose, that's perfectly okay."

Ranjana was giving me permission to stay stuck. She was giving me the heads up to be miserable. No one had EVER given me that kind of acceptance before. My whole life I had been taught to do better, be better, be stronger, be something else, anything else than what you are. But acceptance... this was a whole new adventure all of its own. I had to really sit with this, integrate this and most of all digest this. Self-acceptance wasn't in my language. It also wasn't in my knowledge. What an eye-opener! I've always accepted everyone for who they are, but I'd never accepted myself or had that acceptance from anyone else. I had this deep core belief that I would never be enough for anyone, and I would have to always give more than I would ever get back. The acceptance I had here was that I was worthless and everyone else was worthy. Damn… I had to change that.

As I became more determined to shift my energy, the deeper I went the stronger the results. The stronger the results, the more liberated I felt. The more liberated I felt, the more empowered I felt. And the strangest part of all was that my behaviour and reactions were changing. My fear levels were reducing. PTSD reactions were less intense, in fact some situations weren't bothering me at all. My anxiety was reduced to the point I was sleeping and eating again.

Could this really be true?! I remember a few times I would try and feel the reactions I would normally have, and I couldn't.

So, there is something in this Emotional Freedom Technique. It really does rewire your brain to think more clearly and be more at peace! It's quite heavenly, you know. To be able to no longer be a victim to the trauma you've been through or the drama of what ifs that keep you awake until 4am.

This was one reason why I created the '28 days to personal power' programme to enable my clients to create a daily habit of tapping… with a belly full of empowerment thrown in. I still believe to this day, if someone shows you how to reclaim your power, grab it with both hands and stick at it like glue.

It's so easy to empower others, but when your life is filled with self-doubt, unworthiness, lack of self-love, rejection, abandonment, abuse and trauma, it can feel almost impossible to empower yourself. So, if you ever feel that way, I want you to know that it's perfectly okay to feel that way and it won't last! That's a promise. Think of it this way, it's just energy in motion!

Now that I had embarked on this journey to shift my energy to the point I was beginning to see my own worth, it was time for another level up – to do something that almost fitted in with a midlife crisis!

My journey progressed, and I soaked it all up like a sponge, with sheer tenacity and determination to create empowered change in my life. It was time for the next step! I did NOT see this one coming, just so you know. It wasn't part of the plan. But, it made my new life plan even more exciting, liberating and beyond anything I had ever known… FREEDOM was mine.

One of my friends, Warren, popped over, and he said, "I've got a new toy, can I show you?" I knew exactly what he meant, but I wanted to wait and see if I got it right, as I was still doubting myself. He rocked up at the door and I heard the engine before I heard him… he walked in, and I said I knew it!

It turned out, although we'd been friends for almost a year, I never knew he was a biker. I LOVED BIKES! Always had. Always will. So, of course, my natural reaction was, "When are you taking me out?!"

His face lit up! He said, "I did wonder if you liked bikes, but I had no idea you loved bikes, get yourself some gear and I'll take you out!"

I waited and waited, but my patience was wearing thin… and I just had this thought: Why the fuck are you waiting for someone to give you something you want?! Learn to ride your own, Vicki. You won't regret it!

And so I did! I made that decision and without a doubt. It all happened, the universe wanted me to have this amazing adventure and so it brought it to me. I was guided to a bingo hall evening with one of my best friends, where I won the jackpot. This covered the price of the bike, my own gear and lessons, training and tests! My first ever experience of manifesting what I wanted in my life! Without knowing how! It just happened.

Within a matter of fourteen days of making this decision, I had the cash and booked a CBT to start my journey.

You might be thinking why does any of this matter? Let me explain. Never in my entire life had I had a hobby of my own until this point.

I worked hard, studied, grew, tried to keep fit even, but I had NEVER had a hobby that I could enjoy for just me. I didn't believe I was worthy of time for myself, fun, adventure or anything that didn't relate to kids, house, work, relationship. I would always feel guilty if I wanted to do something for myself. But then that was more to do with the relationship I was in and the mindset of 'putting everyone first' so I could simply live in peace – I had to open up to this being my new 'normal'.

So here I am, this woman who is 5'0 with suddenly every other weekend to herself to play around on this bike! Off to play I went.

I took my bike for her first little cake and tea run. We (me and my bike are a 'we' now!) went to the 1066 café. I was prepared. A simple ride in, no gravel for me to worry about and a simple ride out. I've got this! As I approached my bike, I had a sick feeling… the fear, the worry, the angst, and I made a promise to myself in that moment: "I will defeat this, and I will overcome this panic and anxiety!" In my heart I knew, if I was going to continue this journey, I would need to increase my confidence and fast.

Everyone will experience anxiety in some form when starting something new. It's a comfort zone thing. The ego in all its glory, whilst its job is to keep you safe. It makes you feel afraid, even in the slightest moments. One thing I teach my clients is to remember the time you first made a cuppa. It takes practice to get it right and the more you do it the less you have to think about it, it just becomes a habit. So, that's what I planned to do next. Make my bike journey a natural habit.

Every single day for six weeks, I got out on that bike even if it was just for an hour. I made a point of going out and riding. Until I no longer felt sick getting on that bike. I ventured wider and further and kept stretching my limits, my distance and growing my skills and ability. I was lucky enough to be making new friends with this new hobby too. Warren was a superstar through it all; he would come out with me just to make sure I was safe, he would keep me company and supported me throughout. I remember one day I was adamant I was going out, whether it rained or not, and he committed to coming with me, but there was a compromise needed. We would have to go and get some new waterproofs to go over the leathers!

As my journey began with this newfound hobby, my whole life began to change. I was evolving with the foundations of a new career but also evolving with my first ever hobby!

March 2018 came around fast and furious. I was told that in forty-eight hours I wouldn't have my girls for five days, basically they weren't being brought home. So, I just sat there and thought oh okay, what the hell am I going to do with myself for five days?

My biggest adventure in life was about to commence! I decided to travel to Land's End and have a SOLO two-wheeled adventure. This again may not seem that much of a big deal to some, but to me this was huge.

Let's recap here. Three years prior to this point in my life, I was an empty worthless shell of a human. No energy, an autoimmune disease, PTSD, severe anxiety, stress-related depression and so much more. In those three years, I had been away for a weekend with a friend to Spain, I'd gone on a camping weekend, and I'd completed the Filthy Girl Mud Run on my own in Derby! I drove all the way to Derby on my own, pitched up a tent in a field with thousands of other women and I knew no one! It was an amazing weekend, and I made some new friends too.

This next adventure was about to be the icing on the cake. A solo adventure indeed. It was also a way for me to deal with the grief of losing my gran three weeks prior. But, actually, it was just the universe giving me a nudge to move forward with one more step, live my life and grow my confidence that little bit more.

I still have the article I wrote about riding 1000 miles on my own with a whole community of women cheering me on, meeting me at difference places en route and offering me a place to stay! It was magical! I never did publish the article, but I still have it as a reminder for what I can do when I put my mind to it.

In fact, in three years, I had started learning more about me than I had ever known, and piece by piece, day by day, the fire in my belly started burning that little bit brighter. I was able to finally look in the mirror and not hate what was reflected back at me. I was able to feel my fear but know I could handle whatever life threw at me. I was becoming stronger, more empowered, more liberated, and more ME! Alongside my healing journey and hobbies, etc., I took up another self-care activity.

This was super cool… suddenly I had hobbies, a life to live and a brand new me to explore!

There was something very important about this journey, that I really want to share with you. Because I know you can massively benefit from this. (Whether now or when you are ready. You will know when you are ready for this.)

It was January 2018 and, after being told and told and told to start journaling, I knew it was something I had to do.

So here we go, full on *Bridget Jones* style! (If you haven't watched it, I recommend you do and keep playing it on repeat until you can laugh no more!)

I was ready to embrace this journey. Page 1: I wrote down my age, left out the weight! Who cares about that anyway, right?! I wrote down my current happiness score and I just wrote about how my day had been. I added in a little bit of gratitude and then closed it up.

I was abso-freaking-lutely clueless, as I sat questioning myself. Is this how you are supposed to journal? Is this what a journal is? I felt a bit awkward as I really didn't know what I was doing. But, I didn't give up, I persevered. In a matter of weeks, my journal game was on fire! I started writing about things that I was feeling, questioning, confused and bewildered by. I would write about the motions of the day. I would write about the funny things the kids said or did. I would write about my friendships, my adventures. I started writing as if it was my best friend.

Journaling was a massive part of my healing journey for many reasons, but one reason I really want you to take note of here, as I know this may seem like a foreign language right now, but journaling taught me to trust myself.

The more I wrote, the more time passed, the more I was able to see that I wasn't wrong (well, not all the time)! I was, in fact, highly intuitive and my predictions and perceptions were on point, even when they were denied by others.

If there is one thing you can do for yourself, it's to learn how to trust yourself. Some people may say it's to

191

love yourself, and I agree that this is super-duper important (I've even created a course on self-love). But, when you trust yourself, you learn to love yourself naturally.

Self-trust is the key to unlocking the brain, to empowering confidence and self-belief to follow your heart and create the life you truly want to live, and I cannot rate journaling enough for you to do just that, especially as a starting point.

Self-doubt was a huge part of the abuse I had suffered. I was coerced to believe that it was 'all in my head' but when I began journaling and learning to trust myself, as well as using EFT and Reiki, this was my recipe for self-healing. I hope you can find some inner strength to give it a go! It's also a subconscious healing technique, so you are healing your life by letting that pen flow. It's also a great sleep provider. Write everything, get it all out... and sleep!

So, whilst we are on the topic of journaling, here are some journaling prompts to help you take a step forward into your next chapter... because you are the one that has the power to tune into your heart and create it now.

Use this space to journal:

Journal questions:

1. What does your life look like when you have reached that place of happiness and contentment? Who's with you, what are you doing? Where are you going? What's surrounding you? Can you see anything specific? Allow your mind to flow and dream. Visualise and write.

2. If you could have ONE hobby right now, what would it be and why?

3. If you could shift your energy by waving a magic wand, what would you change?

4. If you had zero limits or restrictions on your life, where would you be five years from now?

5. Can you write about five things you have been grateful for in the last few days?

_____

_____

_____

_____

_____

_____

_____

_____

More to her Life charity

She sits alone on her bed in the dark, her children softly sleeping next to her and wonders, "What now??!"
What will become of her life? She fears she is not strong enough to provide for herself and her children.
It is at this point she decides to return to her abusive partner.

This is why More to her Life was created, to show her how incredible life will be away from abuse and that she has the power to create it, so she never makes that decision.

This book was published by More to her Life charity (registered charity number 1191910) and the aim of this book directly echoes the work the charity does.

More to her Life charity supports women who have experienced domestic abuse by delivering gifts and experiences designed to show them how incredible life can be away from abuse. More to her Life was founded by Victoria Padmore in November 2020.

Women escaping domestic abuse often have lost their individuality, they have lost touch with themselves. The ability to focus on their own wants and desires have been suppressed throughout the relationship. This is years, sometimes decades of suppression.

They have forgotten how to dream of or design a future they would want to live. They are now faced with trying to rebuild their life, possibly without even knowing what they want that life to look like.

An unknown future is terrifying for anyone and More to her Life is designed to help women see how amazing life can be away from abuse.

By working in connection with other domestic abuse charities, we can ensure their basic human needs are met and they are safe. It is then time for More to her Life to add the next layer of support and give these women a glimpse of the life they deserve!

In our first year we have:
- Helped a woman see the fun she can have with her teenage son by sending them to a water park for the day.
- Helped fourteen women create the Christmas they wanted for them and their children by delivering gift vouchers.
- Gifted a brand new cooker, fridge/freezer and washing machine to a woman moving out of a refuge, as all this was missing in a flat she moved into.
- Sent gift vouchers to many women who also needed or wanted other items and decoration for houses they were moving into after their year in a refuge.
- Helped twenty-eight women to build stronger bonds in the positive relationships in their lives by funding thank you gifts from them to their loved ones.
- Paid for a year-long gym membership for a woman as

she started to focus on her own physical and mental health again.
- Funded a coach trip to the beach for every woman and child living in a refuge.
- And now hopefully inspired thousands of women with this book!

Each and every one of these projects is to show women that this could be their lives away from abuse without the shadow of control and fear. Here is one of the messages we got from a woman who experienced one of these days out:

"The trip to the water park allowed me and my son a bit of normality and freedom to do what WE wanted to do, without there being an issue and a fight. To see him belly laugh like he did, showed me that we can have a normal life where we can enjoy things and not be scared about what might happen all of the time; thank you so much for arranging it for us!"

We have so many more projects planned and will continue to do our upmost to answer requests for help from women building their lives away from abuse.

To see how you can support the charity please visit
www.moretoherlife.co.uk
Please feel free to contact us directly at
hello@moretoherlife.co.uk

Printed in Great Britain
by Amazon